AMISH
WALL QUILTS

15 Brilliant and Beautiful Quilts

RACHEL THOMAS PELLMAN

Martingale™
& COMPANY

CREDITS

President	Nancy J. Martin
CEO	Daniel J. Martin
Publisher	Jane Hamada
Editorial Director	Mary V. Green
Managing Editor	Tina Cook
Technical Editor	Jane Townswick
Copy Editor	Ellen Balstad
Design and Production Manager	Stan Green
Illustrator	Laurel Strand
Assistant Illustrator	Lisa McKenney
Cover and Text Designer	Trina Stahl
Quilt Photographer	Brent Kane
Amish Life Photographer	Dennis Hughes, East Petersburg, PA

Martingale™
& COMPANY

That Patchwork Place®

That Patchwork Place® is an imprint of Martingale & Company™.

Amish Wall Quilts: 15 Brilliant and Beautiful Quilts © 2001 by Rachel Thomas Pellman

© 2001 by Dennis Hughes for the photographs on the following pages: 8, 10,12,13,14,17, 21, 26, 31, 33, 34, 43, 47, 48, 56, 58, 66, 83, 85, 94,106.

Martingale & Company
20205 144th Avenue NE
Woodinville, WA 98072-8478 USA
www.martingale-pub.com

Printed in China
06 05 04 03 02 01   8 7 6 5 4 3 2 1

Library of Congress Cataloging-in-Publication Data

Pellman, Rachel T. (Rachel Thomas)
   Amish wall quilts : 50 brilliant and beautiful quilts / Rachel Thomas Pellman.
      p.   cm.
   Includes bibliographical references.
   ISBN 1-56477-396-5
   1. Patchwork—Patterns.   2. Quilting—Patterns.
3. Quilts, Amish.   4. Wall hangings.   I. Title.

TT835 .P3517 2001
746.46'041—dc21

                                    2001042582

ACKNOWLEDGMENTS

THOUGH IT carries my name as the author, this book bears the mark of scores of quiltmakers, quilt enthusiasts, and quilt scholars whose paths have intersected with mine over many years. All the printed bits of information, the solid how-to tips, and the colorful stories shared within these pages have been pulled together with a continuous thread, much like the making of a quilt.

My love for Amish quilts began when I was invited to join the staff at The Old Country Store in Intercourse, Pennsylvania. It was there that I met dozens of quiltmakers (including Old Order Amish women, non-Amish women, and even a few men), as well as expert craftspeople, who were willing to share their friendship, knowledge, and skills in regard to quiltmaking. I value those relationships and I will always be indebted to the many people who enriched my life by sharing their expertise and their stories.

My association with the store also gave me the privilege of seeing and handling hundreds of antique Amish quilts. In their willingness to make them public, the owners of those quilts (both collectors and individuals who shared family heirlooms) made them a source of pleasure and inspiration for myself and many others. Those quilts, as well as their owners, feel like old friends. I am grateful.

I am grateful to Martingale & Company for their willingness to publish this book, and to my editor, Jane Townswick, who made the book better with her careful scrutiny and sensitive understanding.

I am also thankful for the opportunity to meet with quilt guilds and attend quilt shows across the country. Always I come away inspired and touched by the eagerness of quilters to learn and to share their own insights and techniques. We depend on each other.

My heartfelt thanks to the women who cheerfully and tirelessly made the thousands of tiny hand quilting stitches necessary to complete the projects for this book.

I want to thank our sons, Nathaniel and Jesse, who bring color and whimsy to the patchwork of my life and who are two of my best critics.

Finally, my unending love and thanks to Kenny, my husband and soul mate.

CONTENTS

INTRODUCTION

WHEN I LOOK at antique Amish quilts, it is hard to decide whether I am more drawn to their simplicity or to their daring nature. I love the clean, simple lines, the solid colors, and the repetitive blocks that evoke feelings of calm and quiet. I am also aware of the intense drama created by the riot of colors in unexpected combinations. Antique Amish quilts speak a brave and sturdy language of their own, in a voice that is not stifled by the influences of today's quiltmaking trends or styles. I am fascinated by the strength, stamina, and originality of the many gifted women who found ways to express their own individuality while functioning happily within the constraints of the Amish culture. Antique Amish quilts celebrate this life in community, speaking to the values of sharing and mutuality and to a balance of work and pleasure. They also tell of the security and contentment that can come from being part of a group. These quilts belong to an era of separation and innocence.

I am sometimes saddened when I see quilts made by Amish women today and find that these quilts have lost their distinctive quality. Although the art of quiltmaking continues to thrive in Amish communities, it has become an industry that is largely driven by the demands of the general public. Contemporary Amish quilts reflect the color and pattern preferences of society, changing as quiltmaking trends come and go. While new Amish quilts are both beautiful and well crafted, they also tend to be more predictable and repetitious than the naive, intuitive style of their antique counterparts.

Although it may be impossible to recapture the innocence of early Amish quilts, we can recreate the charm of these vintage masterpieces. This book contains fifteen wall-size replicas of authentic antique Amish quilts in appropriate patterns, proportions, color combinations, and quilting styles. Because Amish women traditionally made bed quilts in sizes that do not fit today's beds, I feel justified in adapting these patterns to wall quilts that capture all the drama, intrigue, and sensitivities of the originals, in a more usable format. In the project sections of this book, you'll find several patterns typical of three Amish regions in the United States: Lancaster County, Pennsylvania; the Midwest; and Mifflin County, Pennsylvania. To make a replica of a typical Lancaster County Amish quilt, choose a Lancaster quilt pattern you like and combine it with any of the Lancaster quilting motifs that appeal to you. You can do the same thing for the midwestern and Mifflin County quilts. Use the quilt comparison chart on page 25 as a helpful overview of colors typically favored by each Amish community as you gather fabrics for your quilts.

My hope is that you will use this book as a guidebook, rather than as a rulebook, and bring your imagination and a sense of adventure to making quilts that reflect both traditional Amish styles and your own personal preferences.

Happy stitching!

Rachel Thomas Pellman

Rhythms of Amish life are closely tied to the cycles of the seasons.
Carefully tended fields and gardens yield bountiful produce, which is received as a gift from God.

AMISH HISTORY

THE BEGINNINGS OF the Amish faith and culture occurred during the Protestant Reformation in sixteenth-century Europe, where the beliefs of the Catholic church were being challenged. The Anabaptist (meaning re-baptizer) movement began in Zurich, Switzerland, in 1525 and spread rapidly into Germany, France, and the Netherlands. Interpreting the Bible for themselves, this group of radical young reformers spoke for a strong separation of church and state. They believed that baptism and church membership were not choices that any child could make. They renounced infant baptism and promoted voluntary adult baptism instead. Using the life of Jesus as their model, they also refused to take oaths, and, believing in nonresistance, rejected military conscription as well.

The state persecuted the Anabaptists severely, torturing and killing thousands of people in an agonizing period that is graphically detailed in the book *Martyrs Mirror* by Thieleman J. van Braught, published in 1660. The Mennonites, a group that the Amish were at first a part of, originated in this Anabaptist movement. The name *Mennonite* was derived from one of the group's prominent leaders—Menno Simmons. In 1693, some of the Mennonites decided to split from the group. Several issues were at stake, but church discipline became a particularly troublesome concern. This group was led by Mennonite church leader Jacob Amman, who had strong convictions for maintaining the purity of the church. His supporters were eventually called Amish.

The first Amish people came to North America in the mid 1700s, seeking religious freedom and stability. They settled in Pennsylvania. Later, some of these people moved on to establish settlements in Ohio, Indiana, and other areas of the Midwest. The earliest Amish settlements struggled to maintain a sense of community and identity within each group; their numbers were small, families were scattered, and outside influences threatened their solidarity. As Amish families became financially more stable and their numbers increased, these settlements became more cohesive, leading to the well-defined Amish communities known today.

A farm provides opportunities for whole families to work together. Both old and young find fulfillment in being needed. This midwestern family heads for a day at the local market.

AMISH LIFE TODAY
Maintaining Community

LANGUAGE

ONE OF THE important elements in defining and maintaining the structure of Amish communities today is the language they speak. Their German dialect is known as Pennsylvania German, and is often referred to as Pennsylvania Dutch (Deutsche). Amish children learn Pennsylvania Dutch at home and are fluent in their own language before they are taught English. Conversations between Amish people, whether at home or in public, are usually conducted in Pennsylvania Dutch. If an "English" (non-Amish) person is part of the group, they switch to English so that everyone can be included. Outsiders eavesdropping on Pennsylvania Dutch conversations often recognize a generous sprinkling of English words.

Amish children are taught both English and formal German in school; lessons are conducted in English, although in casual conversation, students may revert to the Pennsylvania Dutch language used at home. The Amish songbook is written in formal, or high German. Formal German is also used for scripture readings. The boundary established by this shared language is powerful, creating a very clear sense of who is part of the group and who is not.

"Consider the lilies of the field, how they grow; they toil not, neither do they spin: And yet I say unto you, that even Solomon in all his glory was not arrayed like one of these."
Matthew 6:28–29

DRESS

ANOTHER CLEAR LINE of distinction between Amish and non-Amish people is clothing. Amish women dress simply and modestly, wearing solid-colored dresses that have uncomplicated lines. The upper part of an Amish dress is often covered with a loose-fitting cape, which is made with the same upper dress fabric. A woman drapes the cape over her shoulders and attaches it at the waistline, providing even more modesty. Other wardrobe staples include an apron, black stockings, and black shoes. An adult woman's hair is uncut and worn parted in the middle, pulled back, twisted into a bun, and covered by a handmade, organdy prayer covering. This tradition is based on the New Testament teachings in I Corinthians 11, which says that a woman's head should be covered for prayer and to symbolize her

Though uniform in style, Amish dresses exhibit great color variety.
This wash line indicates a family with lots of girls in a range of sizes.

acceptance of God's authority. At home, Amish women often wear dark kerchiefs or scarves tied around their heads, rather than organdy coverings. For formal occasions, the white organdy cap is traditional. A heavy protective bonnet is worn over the covering outdoors. Jewelry and makeup are not part of an Amish woman's lifestyle.

Amish men also dress distinctively, in broadfall pants, solid-colored shirts for daily wear or white shirts for dress, suspenders, and wide-brimmed hats. The hat is a distinguishing symbol for an Amish man; it is consistently worn outdoors for both casual and formal occasions. Hat types change with the seasons; black felt is favored in cold months, while straw hats are worn in warmer weather. For church and other formal occasions, men wear black "plain" suits without lapels, which feature hook-and-eye closures

rather than buttons. Men's hair is worn cropped at the neckline and parted in the middle. Before he marries, an Amish man is clean-shaven; after marriage, he shaves his upper lip and allows his beard to grow long and remain untrimmed. If an Amish man does not marry, he will eventually grow a beard.

Amish children's garments make them look much like miniature adults; however, the solid colors of their clothing are often brighter, livelier colors than the adults'. This difference in color is especially easy to see in the bright blue and purple bonnets often worn by younger girls. Very young girls wear prayer coverings only for church or special occasions, and not to school until they reach seventh or eighth grade. Boys begin wearing hats at an early age, and by the time they go to school, hats are a part of their outdoor apparel.

EDUCATION

AMISH CHILDREN LEARN the basics of reading, writing, and arithmetic in private, one-room schools, where classes are taught by people who have strong academic abilities. Within the Amish culture, life skills are as valued as academic knowledge. While there is high worth placed on learning, the Amish believe that too much education is somewhat suspect. Amish children receive formal education only through the eighth grade; after that, life teaches its own lessons.

CHURCH

RATHER THAN GATHERING together in church buildings, Amish people worship in private homes. Meetings are held every other Sunday and they move from home to home within Church districts, which are organized by considering both numbers of people and location. Church membership is voluntary and occurs when a child is capable of making that choice on his or her own. It is easy to assume that because a child grows up surrounded and immersed in Amish culture, he or she may not really have a choice about joining the church. However, Amish children are like children everywhere; they ask questions, live on the edge, and experiment with things that make parents uncomfortable. Although some children do leave the communities in which they grew up, 80 percent or more decide to stay within the group, which speaks very well for the stability, comfort, and contentment in the Amish culture. It is not a perfect group; there are unhappy marriages, unsettled minds, unsuccessful workers, and unhealthy babies. However, the underlying support system encourages healthy, wholesome relationships, and surrounds and comforts people when things go wrong. In Amish culture, everyday existence and the rhythms of life are accepted as gifts from God. The Amish believe it is enough simply to accept that certain events take place; they don't need to understand why. This acceptance is not the result of ignorance or small-mindedness; rather, it is a choice the Amish make to submit to nature and to the dictates and decisions that best serve the group. In Amish culture, the concept of "we" is much more valued than "I."

LIMITING TECHNOLOGY

AMISH CULTURE RESTRICTS the influence of the outside world. As a general rule, their homes do not have electricity, although this does not mean that they live without modern conveniences. Diesel-fueled generators provide pneumatic, hydraulic, and belt power to equipment and appliances around the house, farm, and shop. Looking remarkably similar to those of their non-Amish neighbors, Amish homes hold stoves, refrigerators, blenders, coffeemakers, and sewing machines.

Two major elements that are missing from the

Straw hats and bare feet are typical for little boys in summertime.

Amish family scene are radio and television. The absence of these powerful media gives Amish people a great deal of control over the information that comes into the home. Amish people enjoy reading and often visit public libraries, selecting books with wholesome, educational value, and periodicals such as *National Geographic* or its youthful counterpart, *Ranger Rick.* Many families also eagerly await the delivery of the local daily newspaper and read copies of the *Budget,* a weekly newspaper from Sugarcreek, Ohio, that caters to the interests of Amish and Mennonite communities throughout North America.

Although regulations vary somewhat from one region to another, most Amish homes have strict guidelines regarding telephones and computers. With the increase in cottage industry among the

"Honour thy father and mother."
Ephesians 6:2

Amish today, telephones have become almost a necessity. Most phones are installed in a barn, workshop, or a little phone booth some distance from the house. Many telephones are equipped with answering machines that take calls and make it possible to run a business without being ruled by it. This compromise of technology and restriction may not be as efficient as today's corporate businesses, but for the most part, it works well.

Cell phones have created a whole new dilemma for the Amish. Originally, their cautions against phones and electricity were based on the obvious connections to outside society. While cell phones are not literally connected, they have caused concerns because of their potential for interrupting family life. The Amish may be several steps ahead of

Horse-drawn carriages are the primary mode of travel for Amish families.
At this pace there is time to enjoy the sights and smells along the way.

general society, which is only now beginning to question whether cell phones should be permitted in restaurants, places of entertainment, and cars because of their distracting quality.

Computers are another knotty issue for the Amish. While some businesses use them for bookkeeping and desktop publishing, some major questions surround them. The Amish do not see technology as a bad thing in itself, but they wish to make changes by choice rather than by default. Therefore, new concepts, tools, and technologies must be processed and examined for their potential effects on individuals as well as the entire group.

TRANSPORTATION

THE MOST COMMON method of travel for an Amish family is a horse and carriage. At such a slow travel pace, there is actually time to see one's surroundings. When it's cold outside, they can bundle up, and in hot weather, the air conditioner is the breeze flowing through the open buggy. Amish people view a horse not only as a worker but also as a friend. Horses are fed and cared for the way one protects a sound and valuable asset. Cars are not seen as inherently evil; Amish people do hire drivers and travel by car whenever the need arises, such as a trip to the doctor or to visit a family member in another part of the county. By hiring a driver, they are able to take advantage of the convenience while avoiding a temptation to "run around." For the Amish, being at home is the norm rather than the exception, and they work together to maintain their farms and family businesses.

"Who can find a virtuous woman? for her price is far above rubies. The heart of her husband doth safely trust in her, so that he shall have no need of spoil. She will do him good and not evil all the days of her life."
Proverbs 31:10–12

MEN'S AND WOMEN'S ROLES

THE AMISH SOCIAL system is a patriarchal one, in which men make the decisions that govern both church and family life. The identity of an Amish woman may seem to be swallowed up when she marries; for example, if Lydia's husband's name is John, she may come to be known as "John's Lydia" or "John Lydia." Yet this is not a culture where women are oppressed; rather, there is a great deal of respect between the genders. Men become deeply involved in the daily care and teaching of children, and it is not uncommon for men to be accompanied by their sons or daughters as they go about their daily chores. On an Amish farm, working together is paramount, and the lines between men's work and women's work can become blurred. Amish women often help with fieldwork and milking, and men feel at ease working in the garden. A whole family might enjoy sitting together to peel peaches or shell beans for canning and freezing. Meal preparation and housecleaning, however, typically fall to women. Amish men respect and appreciate the effort and ability required in keeping a household functional.

Creating a comfortable space that is clean and inviting is an ongoing source of deep satisfaction for many Amish women, who feel a sense of companionship from knowing that their peers share the same lot in life. However, these are not "stamp-pad" women who all look and act alike; each is an individual with distinct preferences and personality. Working within community boundaries gives Amish women a freedom and relaxation that their non-Amish counterparts sometimes do not feel. Submission by women to men is taught as a biblical principle. At its worst, this can create control and abuse. At its best, it creates mutual service and love. In marriage, both men and women gain a companion, a helper, and a friend.

Single life is the exception rather than the norm among the Amish, but it may be more comfortable and fulfilling within Amish circles than it is in general society. Single women caring for aging parents or teaching school, for example, are regarded with dignity and respect, and extended family living arrangements make it possible to incorporate single women and men as part of the whole.

The Amish accept the end of life as a natural passage. While they are not opposed to modern medicine or hospitals and use both when required, elderly family members are not usually placed in retirement homes or nursing care facilities to die. Rather, the family rallies around and provides care in the home, keeping the patient comfortable and in familiar surroundings as they face the uncertainties of death. Life is highly valued, but it is not usually sustained with all the fervor of available technology. Death is as real as life to the Amish, and the pain of separation is eased by their belief that after death comes new life in heaven, where loved ones will eventually be reunited.

SHARED GENERATIONS

THE MOTTO "EARLY to bed and early to rise" is still followed by Amish families today. Perhaps their closeness to the land makes them more aware of the natural rhythms of the earth. When the sun goes down and night falls, it is time to rest. With the rising of the sun, there is another day in which to be productive. Fortified with a hearty breakfast, both children and the older generations work together in the daily routines of farm life. Using horses and mules rather than large tractors means that farms stay relatively small. The addition of a *Dawdy* house, or grandfather's house, as an extension to the larger farmhouse makes it possible for the younger generation to live and work on the farm without forcing the older generation to leave. Everyone is valued for their roles: little children and elderly grandparents help with the lighter chores, and the heavier work is left to the more robust family members.

"To every thing there is a season, and a time to every purpose under the Heaven."

Ecclesiastes 3:1

BEAUTY AND FUNCTION

QUILTMAKING COMBINES TWO qualities that are highly esteemed by the Amish: beauty and function. While simplicity and austerity characterize their lives, Amish people have always had a great appreciation for beauty. The splendor of a beautiful sunrise or sunset is not lost on these people, whose daily rhythms are bonded with the earth and the beauty of each passing season. The soil they till to produce food is also cultivated to grow beautiful flowers.

The Amish admire and enjoy lovely objects because of their usefulness, regarding beauty with caution only when it is connected to pride. For example, Amish homes have an abundance of fancy dishes; beautifully painted furniture; elaborate, handwritten family records; and hand-embroidered linens. The pleasure that comes from owning these objects is enhanced because of their decorative quality, and yet that beauty in itself is

*Little children learn many of life's lessons
by watching and listening.*

QUILTING AS A CREATIVE OUTLET

MOST AMISH WOMEN are skilled enough at sewing to provide basic clothing for the family. Not every Amish woman enjoys working with a needle and thread; for some, home sewing is a chore. Even for those who do enjoy sewing, constructing clothing offers little creative opportunity. The church limits the variations allowed in women's clothing styles; while sizes differ and change, the patterns remain basically the same, and the only fabric options are solid colors. Any satisfaction that comes from sewing clothing is likely to be from having done a job well rather than following a creative urge.

Quiltmaking, however, offers a multitude of creative options in regard to patterns, colors, and designs. Antique Amish quilts feature only solid colors, but the possibilities for unique color combinations are virtually limitless. Although the widespread use of particular patterns in certain Amish regions suggests that some designs were more acceptable than others, early Amish quilts featured many pattern variations. For example, a Center Diamond pattern might be made with or without inner borders, with or without corner blocks, or feature straight or sawtooth edges. Occasionally, the center diamond was also broken into small blocks to form a Sunshine and Shadow pattern within the diamond shape. For early Amish women, quiltmaking was an open arena for creativity and self-expression within the boundaries set by the church, and it is the same in Amish groups today.

only secondary. Without functionality, the value of these objects would be lost to the Amish. Quilts fit very well into this mind-set because they are both beautiful and functional at the same time. Many surviving antique Amish quilts never saw much daily use; rather, they were often stored in blanket chests for many years and brought out only to admire or serve as bed coverings for special occasions. And yet, these people would not have hesitated to use their quilts daily if necessary.

Center Diamond quilt, circa 1925. Made by a member of the Benuel King family,
southern Lancaster County. Wool top, cotton batting, cotton backing, 75" x 75".
Collection of the Heritage Center of Lancaster County.

ANTIQUE AMISH QUILTS

NAIVE BEAUTY

ANTIQUE AMISH QUILTS show a great deal of freedom and abandon in their color schemes. Perhaps it is this naive approach to color that makes these quilts so special. Early Amish women did not live in isolation from the outside world; they interacted with their non-Amish neighbors, saw Sears and Roebuck catalogs, and were aware of fashion and fabric trends. However, these things had minimal influence on their personal lives. The walls in their homes were painted a solid color (often pale blue or green), and window treatments were simple pull blinds. If there was carpet on the floor, it was usually a woven rag rug, and there was virtually no upholstered furniture. In most aspects of their lives, early Amish women had little need to exercise their abilities in regard to combining colors. But quiltmaking was different. The quilts they made featured startling color placements in bold and daring combinations. Uninhibited by any formal knowledge of color theory, these Amish women simply followed their hearts. Anything was an option; they used unlikely fabric blends together and watched them come alive in their quilts. It would be misleading to suggest that all early Amish quilts were successful; some were down-right ugly.

In general, cultural boundaries seemed only to inspire and liberate early Amish quiltmakers rather than hem them in, and they created classic masterpieces with timeless appeal that ranged from traditional to what is considered modern art today. It is ironic that antique Amish quilts, which came from a culture that valued humility and simplicity, are sought-after as art objects today. Antique Amish quilts hang on museum walls and decorate upscale corporate offices in many parts of the country. Although the quilts are beautiful in these settings, it is important to remember that their creators saw themselves as quiltmakers, not quilt artists. Viewed with an understanding of the Amish culture, these quilts embody the values of commitment, discipline, simplicity, and belonging that have always been important to the Amish way of life.

QUILTING FEEDS THE SOUL

IT IS EASY to see from the styles of the quilting designs in antique Amish quilts that quilting went far beyond the functional purpose of anchoring the three layers of a quilt "sandwich" (top, batting, and backing) together. A pieced quilt top with plain borders was an open canvas for Amish women to stitch lavish, intricate quilting designs. At an Amish quilting bee, up to fifteen women often gathered around a floor frame large enough to stretch a full-size bed quilt. As they stitched, they shared common dreams and goals, joys and difficulties, and cemented friendships. Stitching in a group offered an opportunity to interact with other generations; young Amish women could sit for hours, talking with their mothers, aunts, grandmothers, and friends, learning important life lessons. And little children, playing near the frame, absorbed volumes about what would be expected of them as adults. In this setting, quilting reinforced and reestablished the values of being Amish.

SETTLEMENT REGIONS

AMISH WOMEN DID not arrive in North America bearing trunkloads of exceptional quilts. Most likely they learned the art of quiltmaking from their non-Amish neighbors after they arrived. The earliest known dated Amish quilt is from the year 1849. There is little evidence of much quiltmaking activity among Amish women before the late 1800s to early 1900s. When they began, however, Amish women made quilts in earnest and even the earliest Amish quilts indicate that these women were quite at home with needle and thread. The hallmark period for antique Amish quilts is generally from 1900 to 1940, when Amish women made quilts of masterpiece quality in color, design, and workmanship.

Antique Amish quilts are generally grouped into three regional categories that outline the geography of Amish settlements in the late nineteenth and early twentieth centuries: Lancaster County, the Midwest, and Mifflin County. Lancaster County in southeastern Pennsylvania was among the earliest Amish settlements. Migration to Mifflin County in central Pennsylvania and the midwestern states, including Indiana, Ohio, Illinois, and Iowa, followed. Though some characteristics were shared across these groups, there were also distinctive features in each one. There were no written rules about what could or could not be done in making quilts; however, there did seem to

be some unwritten understanding about what was acceptable and what was not in each region.

FAVORITE PATTERNS

THE FOLLOWING QUILT patterns are typical of the early quilts made in each of the three Amish regions of the United States.

Lancaster County

In general, Lancaster County quilts were square with wide borders (12" to 15" for full-size quilts), and they often featured corner blocks in both the inner and outer borders. The bindings on these quilts were wide.

The Center Diamond (or Diamond-in-a-Square) pattern shown on page 36 was used over and over by Lancaster County Amish quilters but seldom by other Amish communities. The large center square was set on-point to form the center diamond and enclosed by an inner border or left to float by itself on surrounding triangles. The Sawtooth Diamond pattern, a variation of the Center Diamond pattern, set the center diamond within a framework of tiny triangles, creating a jagged sawtooth edge all around it.

Bars, a pattern of simple vertical strips (page 40), was another favorite among Lancaster County quiltmakers. They often created variations of it by splitting the bars into triple bands of color or by setting rows of another pieced block such as a Nine Patch or Flying Geese within the vertical bars.

The Sunshine and Shadow pattern on page 50 creates the illusion of light and dark with bands of color that radiate around the center in rows of small squares. This familiar design is often known as Trip around the World when done in printed fabrics. The solid colors used by Amish quilters produced a dramatic, gradual flow from light to dark. Although women in other Amish communities sometimes used this pattern, Sunshine and Shadow is most often associated with the Lancaster County Amish.

The Nine Patch pattern often became a Double Nine Patch (page 44) in the hands of Lancaster County Amish women. They liked to set small nine-patch units together to form larger blocks with nine sections. Then they would set these blocks against plain blocks; hence, the name Double Nine Patch. The smaller nine-patch units were often made in many different colors, creating the effect of color sparkling throughout the quilt.

The Triple Irish Chain pattern (page 54), a simple and graceful pattern that features squares in a continuous chain-like effect across the surface of a quilt, was also commonly used in the Lancaster region. Other popular patterns among Lancaster County Amish quiltmakers included Lone Star (page 60), Baskets (page 76), Fan, and Crazy Patch. (For quilts that feature Fan and Crazy Patch patterns, see *The World of Amish Quilts* and *A Treasury of Amish Quilts*. Reference information is available on page 128.)

The Midwest

Antique midwestern Amish quilts were generally rectangular, with borders that were proportionately narrower (5" to 8" for full-size quilts) than Lancaster County quilts, and with fewer corner blocks. Bindings on these quilts were narrow.

Midwestern Amish women often chose fancy inner borders, sometimes combining a pieced inner border with a plain outer border. These quiltmakers were more influenced by quilt patterns and styles of the non-Amish people than the Lancaster County quilters were. Common pattern choices included Ocean Waves (page 68), Bear's Paw (page 72), Baskets (page 76), Ohio Star (page 80), Monkey Wrench (page 86), and Shoofly (page 90). Midwestern Amish quilts most often featured a series of repeated blocks, set against plain blocks or directly against another pieced block that sometimes formed a secondary pattern at the juncture.

Mifflin County

Early Amish quilts from the Mifflin County region were usually rectangular, with border and binding proportions that were similar to midwestern quilts. Popular patterns seemed to stem from variations of simple Four Patch or Nine Patch blocks. These smaller blocks were often set together to create larger pieced blocks called *blockwork*. Mifflin County quilts had more of a scrap-quilt look than quilts from other Amish communities, and they were more likely to incorporate a variety of different colored fabrics rather than a unified color palette throughout the design. The most commonly used patterns in Mifflin County were Four Patch (page 96), and Nine Patch in Blockwork (page 100), along with many variations of these patterns. A few other patterns were also used in this region, including some spectacular examples of Log Cabin (page 104).

A young Amish girl waits with a load of cantaloupes for market.

COLOR PALETTES

THE COLORS IN antique Amish quilts were often the same as the ones in the clothing worn by members of the communities where they were made. Here is a look at the color palettes favored by quiltmakers in the three early Amish regions.

Lancaster County

The typical colors preferred by Amish communities in Lancaster County included only the cool half of the color wheel—dark red, purple, blue, and green. Yellow, orange, and bright red were most often avoided by this group. Black was a staple color used in clothing but seldom seen in Lancaster quilts. When it did appear in a quilt, it was used sparingly as an accent rather than as a main color.

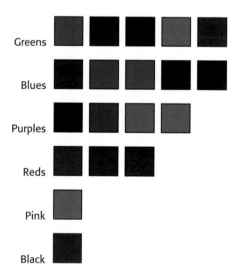

The Midwest

Midwestern Amish women used the entire spectrum of the color wheel, for both their clothing and their quilts. These quiltmakers loved black, often using it as the background for very bright pieced blocks to create dramatic and daring effects in their quilts.

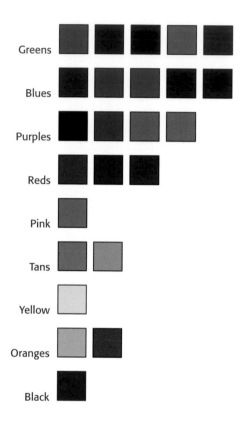

Mifflin County

Quilts from Mifflin County came from two different groups of Amish. The more conservative Nebraska Amish (so called because one of the leaders came from Nebraska) wore largely subdued blues and browns. Quilts from this group reflected those colors, with occasional purples, pinks, and additional dull colors thrown in. The other Mifflin County group made very playful and vibrant quilts, featuring the full range of the color wheel and at times selecting the most daring of hues possible.

More Conservative Color Palette (Nebraska Amish)

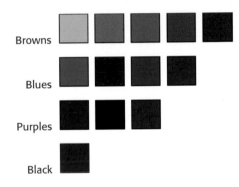

Less Conservative Color Palette

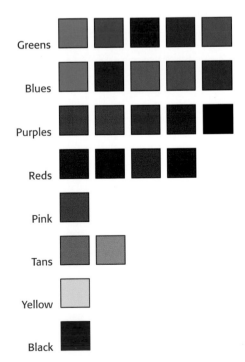

FABRIC CHOICES

ANOTHER WAY TO distinguish between antique quilts from different Amish communities is to discover which types of fabrics were typically used or avoided in each area.

Lancaster County

Financial stability gave Lancaster County Amish women the means to use some of the best fabrics available for their quilts. Both quilt tops and dresses were constructed of fine wool in rich blues, wines, greens, and purples. Wool was the fabric of choice for most quilts until about 1935, when synthetics became more popular for their accessibility and easy care. Quilt backings (sometimes solid colors, sometimes prints) were most often cotton, or on occasion, cotton flannel.

The Midwest

Most quilt tops from the midwestern Amish communities were made of cotton. Lustrous cotton sateen was very popular, producing a shimmering effect in quilts. Quilt backings in the Midwest were also typically made of cotton in solid colors.

Mifflin County

Mifflin County quiltmakers were probably the most carefree of all Amish groups, creating quilt tops made of cotton, with a wide variety of fabrics that produced a scrap look. Quilt backings were also solid-colored cottons.

QUILTING DESIGNS

EARLY AMISH WOMEN were excellent quilters, who lavished their quilts with tiny stitches that flowed effortlessly around deep curves and sharp angles in ornate quilting designs. Quiltmakers in each region showed distinct preferences in regard to the types of quilting motifs they used.

Lancaster County

As a general rule, Lancaster County quilters focused less energy on piecework and more on quilting. Two things probably enhanced the quality of the quilting in Lancaster County quilts. First, wool fabric needled very easily. Second, many Lancaster quilts contained a very thin inner layer, such as an old blanket or a piece of cotton flannel. This thin layer made it easier for quilters to create the nearly perfect stitches associated with early Amish quilts. The bold, angular, pieced quilt tops of Lancaster County women were overlaid with soft, curved quilting designs. And the wide outer borders and the open spaces provided by larger pieced patterns were a great canvas for exhibiting the quilting prowess of their makers.

Feathers were some of the most commonly used quilting motifs in Lancaster County. In borders, quilted feathers might extend from each side of a center vein that stretched out and turned back in a graceful loop. At a corner, a feather might take a deep bend and extend in the opposite direction. Occasionally, a corner block might interrupt the feathered motif in a border and feature its own separate quilting design.

Other widely used quilting designs in this region included baskets, grapes and grape leaves, pumpkin seeds, and crosshatching. Early Lancaster County quilts sometimes featured "double" quilting motifs, where shapes, such as a basket, were outlined with two close rows of quilting stitches. Lancaster County quilters often used black thread for quilting, which made their stitches appear almost invisible against the rich colors of their quilts, except for the beautiful relief patterns they produced.

The Midwest

In the Midwest, piecing seemed to take precedence over quilting. This order of importance may have been because pieced blocks offered less space for intricate quilting motifs. The narrow borders favored by midwestern Amish quilters also restricted the use of elaborate quilting designs; nevertheless, they found ways to enhance their patchwork patterns with quilting. Outlining shapes in a pieced block was not necessarily the first choice; these women were just as likely to stitch beautiful quilting motifs right over a pieced pattern. One popular technique was to quilt straight or diagonal lines in double or triple sets; for example, a repeat-block quilt might feature double or triple straight quilting lines over the whole surface.

Borders often featured simple yet elegant cables and fans, or evenly spaced double or triple lines quilted diagonally. In the Midwest, Amish quilters most often stitched feathers as circular motifs on alternate plain blocks between pieced blocks. Dark colors were the most common choices for quilting thread, but light colors and even white were also used occasionally.

Mifflin County

The casual approach that Mifflin County women used in their piecework also carried over to their choices of quilting designs. Early Mifflin County quilts featured simple and open quilting motifs;

the mulberry leaf was frequently featured in borders, and other simple leaf and vine designs were also favored. As in midwestern Amish quilts, cables and fans were common quilting motifs. In a Mifflin County quilt, it was not unusual to find a fan or cable design that ran off the edge of the border. Calculating the placement or size of a quilting motif to make it turn the corner and repeat on the opposite border did not seem to be a high priority in this region. Mifflin County quilters most often chose to use dark colors of thread for quilting.

QUILT COMPARISON CHART

	Lancaster County	The Midwest	Mifflin County
Patterns	Center Diamond Bars Sunshine and Shadow Double Nine Patch Triple Irish Chain Lone Star	Ocean Waves Ohio Star Shoofly Monkey Wrench Baskets Bear's Paw	Four Patch Nine Patch in Blockwork Log Cabin
Colors	Cool half of the color wheel; very little use of black	Entire color spectrum; lots of black—often as background color	Blues, browns, dull purples in more conservative group; entire color spectrum in less conservative group
Quilting Motifs	Feathers Baskets Pumpkin seeds Cross-hatching Grapes and grape leaves	Cables Fans Feather circles Straight lines in double or triple sets	Mulberry leaf Cables Fans Simple leaves and vines

Sunday afternoons provide time for visiting with family, friends, and neighbors.
Traveling might be done by carriage or by foot.

QUILTMAKING BASICS

FABRICS

ANTIQUE AMISH QUILTS were constructed largely of wool and cotton fabrics. Lancaster County quiltmakers often used tightly woven, lightweight wools for the quilt top and cotton fabrics for the quilt backing. Midwestern and Mifflin County quiltmakers used mostly cotton on both the quilt top and back. Cotton sateen (a cotton fabric with a polished appearance like satin) was a favorite with midwestern quilters.

Though it may not be possible to duplicate the old fabrics, you can achieve similar results using high-quality, 100 percent cottons. Choose fabrics that are tightly woven and feel soft to the touch. It is a good idea to prewash fabrics to be certain that they are colorfast. If a fabric continues to lose color after two or three washings, eliminate it as a possibility for use in your quilts and replace it with another choice.

PIECING AND PRESSING GUIDELINES

THERE IS NO substitute for accuracy at every stage of quiltmaking, from rotary cutting to machine piecing, pressing, and quilting. Precision is especially important when working in the small scale required for wall quilts. Use the following guidelines to enjoy piecing and pressing success in making the projects in this book.

- Keep your sewing machine clean and well serviced. Change to a new, sharp needle at the start of each new project.

- Remember the old adage, "Measure twice—cut once!" Make it a habit to measure accurately *before* you rotary cut the pieces for a quilt, and always use the same type of ruler. A difference of even $\frac{1}{32}$" may seem quite small in itself, but when multiplied across the surface of an entire quilt top, it can create noticeable discrepancies in your quilt's dimensions. Pay attention to the way you position the lines of your ruler each time you rotary cut, and place the ruler the same way as you continue cutting pieces for your quilt.

- All of the measurements in this book include a ¼" seam allowance. Before you begin sewing, check the accuracy of your own seam allowance width on a test piece of fabric. It must measure an exact ¼"; if it does not, use a different presser foot on your sewing machine, change needle positions, or place a piece of tape exactly ¼" to the right of the machine's needle as a guide to accurate piecing.

- When working with solid-colored fabrics, it can often be a challenge to tell which is the right and wrong side. If this is important to you, you can mark the wrong side of each piece to maintain consistency throughout your quilt. The other alternative is to sew the pieces together without regard to the right and wrong side of the fabric. Sewing the pieces this way can actually create subtle shading that enhances the overall look of a pieced pattern, rather than detracting from it.

- Use dark gray cotton thread for piecing. This neutral shade seems to recede into many different colors without calling attention to itself, making it possible to sew almost any combination of medium- to dark-colored fabrics together without the thread being visible.

- Chain-piece pieces together whenever possible. Feed pairs of pieces through the sewing machine one after another, snipping them apart only after you have sewn all of the pairs together. For example, when making the Log Cabin pattern on page 104, sew all of the log #1 pieces to the center squares in a series, snip them apart, press the seam allowances, and then proceed to adding log #2 in the same manner.

- Before sewing combined pieces that have "ears" extending beyond the finished seam lines, such as triangles or diamonds, trim away the "ears" before you pin them together.

- Carefully pressed seams are important for maintaining accuracy. In deciding which way to press them, let common sense be your best guide. In general, press seam allowances toward the darker fabric wherever possible. Be aware of where seams will lie in relation to the lines of the quilting designs you want to use, and wherever possible, press the seam allowances away from the quilting areas. When joining pieces, it is easiest to butt seams so that one seam allowance will lie in one direction and the other will lie in the opposite direction. Occasionally, it may be most prudent to press seam allowances open to avoid bulk.

- Pressing should be done gently on a firm surface. Start by pressing seam allowances flat on the wrong side of your work; this will block the seams and keep them correctly positioned. Then press the seam allowances to one side or the other, usually toward the darker fabric unless this will create too much bulk in a single area. Use great care to avoid stretching and distorting the fabrics as you press, and avoid sliding the iron back and forth over a seam allowance, which can cause distortions.

- The project instructions provide specific dimensions for border pieces. However, depending on the measurements of your completed quilt center, you may need to adjust the length of the borders before you sew them to the quilt. Measure the quilt through the center—horizontally and vertically—to determine the border lengths needed.

MARKING QUILTING DESIGNS

THE QUILTING MOTIFS on pages 108–127 are full-size, and each one is labeled as a Lancaster County, midwestern, or Mifflin County design. Choose the designs you want to feature in your quilt and mark them in the following manner.

1. Trace the quilting designs of your choice onto a piece of white paper with a permanent black marking pen for easy visibility. Tape the traced design on top of a flat surface.

Test any fabric-marking pencil you want to use on some scrap fabrics from your actual quilt top before using it to mark your quilting designs.

2. To mark a quilt top with light fabrics, lay the quilt top over the traced quilting design so that it is positioned as you want it to be in your quilt. Using a removable fabric-marking pencil of your choice, mark the quilting design onto the fabric. Press on the pencil just hard enough so that you can see your markings for quilting and remove them easily after you finish.

> *When you mark quilting designs onto the outer borders of a quilt, remember to position the design so that you allow for the ¼" seam allowance needed for attaching the binding at the edges of the quilt.*

3. To mark quilting designs onto dark fabrics, a light table works best. Tape your traced quilting design right side up on top of the light table, and place your quilt top right side up over the quilting design. Use weights or tape to hold the quilt top in place, if necessary. Trace the quilting design onto the fabric with a removable fabric-marking pencil.

BATTING OPTIONS

IN KEEPING WITH the look and feel of antique Amish quilts, battings that are thin and flat are preferable. While cotton battings are frequently both thin and flat, they are quite often dense as well, which can make hand quilting difficult. Because the quilts in this book feature lots of quilting, thin polyester batting that will needle easily and maintain a thin, flat appearance in the finished quilt is preferable. Other options include substituting a layer of prewashed flannel or an old blanket in place of commercial batting. Whatever type of inner layer you choose, it's a good idea to cut it approximately 2" larger on all sides than your quilt top.

BACKINGS

AS FOR BATTINGS, the backings for the quilts in this book should be approximately 2" larger on all sides than the quilt top. For the square Lancaster County quilts, you will need to cut the backing fabric in half from selvage to selvage; trim the selvages from two long edges; and sew the two lengths right sides together. Then you will press the seam open to reduce bulk and make hand quilting easier. For the rectangular quilts in this book, the backings do not need to be pieced.

LAYERING AND BASTING

YOU CAN EITHER baste the three layers of a quilt sandwich together and place them in a quilting hoop, or stretch the layers onto a large floor frame, which sometimes requires no basting. Follow these steps to prepare a quilt sandwich for hand quilting.

1. Place the quilt backing *wrong* side up on top of a smooth, flat surface, such as a floor or a large table.

2. Lay the batting over the quilt backing, gently smoothing out any wrinkled areas.

3. Center the quilt top, *right* side up on top of the batting. The batting and backing fabric should be approximately 2" larger than the quilt top on all sides. Make sure that all 3 layers are smooth and wrinkle-free.

4. Thread a needle with white thread and baste the 3 layers together with large stitches, starting in the center of the quilt and working toward the outer edges. Baste very close to the edge of the border on all 4 sides of the quilt top.

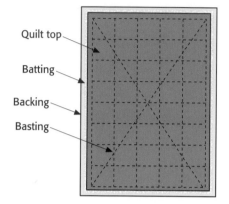

Quilt top

Batting

Backing

Basting

Quilter's rustproof safety pins are an alternative to thread-basting. Look for small ones with narrow shanks that will not leave large holes in the fabric.

HAND QUILTING

THE QUILTING STITCH is a small running stitch that anchors the three layers of a quilt sandwich together securely. To quilt by hand, you will need quilting thread, which is heavier weight than regular sewing thread, and quilting needles called *Betweens.* These needles are short and strong enough to take several stitches at a time through the three layers of a quilt sandwich. Follow these steps to do fine hand-quilting stitches.

1. Thread a quilting needle with a strand of quilting thread approximately 18" to 24" long, and make a small knot at the end of the thread. Insert the needle into the quilt top, about ½" from where you want to start quilting, and bring it out again at the point where you wish to place your first quilting stitch. Gently tug on the thread until the knot "pops" underneath the quilt top and lodges in the layer of batting.

2. With one hand, do small, evenly spaced running stitches along the marked quilting design, moving the needle in an up-and-down rocking motion as you stitch. Hold one finger of your other hand underneath the quilt sandwich so that you can feel the tip of the needle pierce the backing fabric between stitches. When you near the end of the length of thread, make a tiny knot again and "pop" it through the quilt top, hiding it within the batting layer.

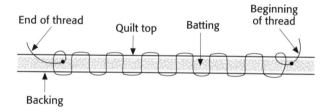

End of thread

Quilt top

Batting

Beginning of thread

Backing

If you do not wish to use a knot at the end of your quilting thread, insert the needle into the quilt top and weave it back through several quilting stitches to secure the end of the thread. Then bring the needle out of the quilt top and clip the thread close to the surface of the fabric.

BINDING A QUILT

THE BINDINGS ON most Amish quilts were applied individually on each side of the quilt, rather than being a continuous binding strip with mitered corners. The following instructions are for binding a quilt in the Amish manner. Refer to the project instructions for the length to cut each binding strip. For the square Lancaster County quilts, you will need to cut eight binding strips and sew them together in pairs, as described below. For the rectangular midwestern and Mifflin County quilts, the binding strips for the top and bottom edges will be single strips without seams, and the binding strips for the sides will be joined in pairs, as for the square Lancaster County quilts.

1. Place 2 binding strips right sides together, with the ends at right angles. Join the strips with a diagonal seam and trim away the excess fabric, leaving a ¼" seam allow-ance. Repeat with the remaining 3 pairs of binding strips, and press the seam allowances open.

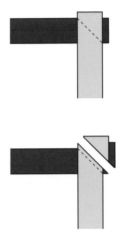

Fieldwork is traditionally done by men, but it is not uncommon for women to be involved—especially during the rush of harvest.

2. Fold the binding strips in half lengthwise, with wrong sides together, and press. Place one of the binding strips at the top edge of the quilt sandwich, with the raw edges even; there will be a bit of excess binding at each end. Sew the binding strip to the top edge of the quilt sandwich.

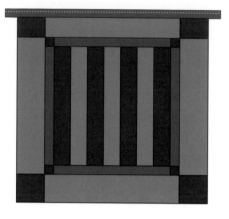

3. Fold the binding up along the seam line, and carefully trim the binding strip even with the sides of the quilt sandwich. Do not bring the binding over to the back side of the quilt at this time; instead, place a pin through all layers to keep the binding folded up. Pinning the binding strip will make it easier to attach the side binding.

Fold straight up.

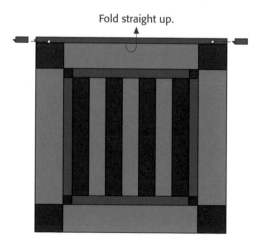

4. Repeat steps 2 and 3 to sew a binding strip to the bottom edge of the quilt sandwich.

5. Referring to steps 1 and 2, sew the 2 remaining binding strips to the sides of the quilt sandwich, taking care to sew all the way across the top and bottom bindings.

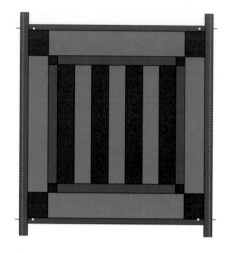

6. Fold over the side binding strips along the seam lines; then carefully trim the side binding strips even with the extended top and bottom binding strips.

7. Bring the top and bottom binding strips around to the back side of the quilt sandwich and whipstitch them to the backing fabric by hand, making sure that the stitching lines are covered.

8. Bring the side binding strips to the back side of the quilt sandwich, creating a fold at each corner. Whipstitch these binding strips to the backing fabric, making sure that the stitching lines are covered.

FINISHING TOUCHES

TO DISPLAY A wall quilt effectively, consider making a hanging sleeve that will accommodate a rod or dowel, which will make the top edge hang perfectly straight. Cut a 4"-wide strip of fabric that is the same length as the top edge of the quilt. Fold the strip in half lengthwise, with wrong sides together, and machine sew a ¼" seam along the long edge. Press this seam open. Turn under a ¼" hem twice at each of the short ends and sew in place. Center the long seam at the middle of the tube of fabric, and press. Stitch the folded edges of the hanging sleeve to the back side of the quilt, just inside the binding.

Amish women sometimes quilted the date (year) and their initials or the initials of the recipient of the quilt into their quilts. For an authentic look, you can do the same, or add a label of your choice with any information you wish to record, such as the name of the quilt, the recipient, or the date you finished the project.

Children are welcomed and loved in Amish circles.
Though they often have daily chores, children also have a
great deal of freedom to play and imagine.

LANCASTER
COUNTY QUILTS

CENTER DIAMOND

BARS

DOUBLE NINE PATCH

SUNSHINE AND SHADOW

TRIPLE IRISH CHAIN

LONE STAR

Rachel Thomas Pellman, 2000, Lancaster, Pennsylvania, 43" x 43".
Quilted by Sadie B. Smoker.

◆

The Center Diamond pattern is a favorite among Lancaster County Amish quilters. Simple geometric shapes provide lots of open space for ornate quilting. This example features traditional feather quilting in the outer border, pumpkin seeds in the inner borders, crosshatching in the triangles, and a feathered circle around an eight-point star in the center.

May 4, 1950

". . . had a quilting on Friday. Eighteen women were present. On Saturday nine girls were here and finished the two quilts."

—From the *Budget*

FABRICS AND SUPPLIES

(fabric 42" wide after prewashing)

♦ 1⅜ yds. green solid for center diamond border, inner border, and binding

♦ ½ yd. burgundy solid for center diamond, center diamond border, inner border, and outer border

♦ ½ yd. medium purple solid for triangles around center diamond

♦ ⅞ yd. dark purple solid for outer border

♦ 2¾ yds. fabric for backing

♦ 47" x 47" piece of batting

CUTTING LIST

All cutting measurements include ¼" seam allowances.

From the green solid, cut:

♦ 4 strips, each 2½" x 15", for center diamond border

♦ 4 strips, each 2½" x 26½", for inner border

♦ 8 strips, each 3¾" x 28", for binding

From the burgundy solid, cut:

♦ 1 square, 15" x 15", for center diamond

♦ 8 squares, each 2½" x 2½", for center diamond border

♦ 4 squares, each 6¾" x 6¾", for outer border

From the medium purple solid, cut:

♦ 2 squares, each 14" x 14". Cut each square in half diagonally to create 4 triangles that will be placed around the center diamond.

From the dark purple solid, cut:

♦ 4 strips, each 6¾" x 30½", for outer border

Assembling the Quilt Top

1. Sew a 2½" x 15" green border strip to 2 opposite sides of the burgundy 15" x 15" center diamond

2. Sew a 2½" x 2½" burgundy square to each end of the remaining two 2½" x 15" green border strips.

3. Sew the border units from step 2 to the remaining sides of the burgundy center diamond to form the center diamond unit.

4. Sew 2 medium purple triangles to opposite sides of the center diamond unit. To be sure that these triangles are properly aligned, fold the center diamond unit in half to find the center point. Then fold the medium purple triangles in half to find their centers. Match and pin the centers of the triangles and the center diamond unit before sewing them together.

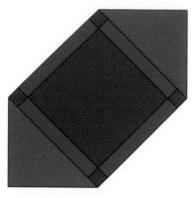

5. Repeat step 4 for the remaining 2 medium purple triangles.

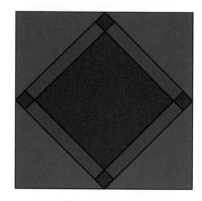

6. Sew two 2½" x 26½" green inner-border strips to the top and bottom edges of the center diamond unit.

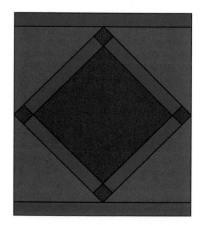

7. Sew a 2½" x 2½" burgundy square to each end of the remaining two 2½" x 26½" green inner-border strips.

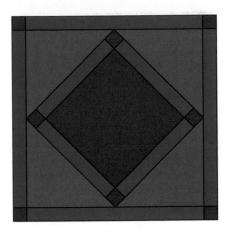

8. Sew the inner-border units from step 7 to the sides of the center diamond unit.

9. Sew a 6¾" x 30½" dark purple outer-border strip to the top and bottom edges of the center diamond unit.

10. Sew a 6¾" x 6¾" burgundy square to each end of the remaining two 6¾" x 30½" dark purple outer-border strips.

11. Sew the outer-border units from step 10 to the sides of the center diamond unit.

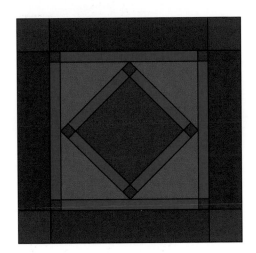

QUILTING AND FINISHING

1. Select the quilting designs from pages 108–127 that you wish to use in your quilt and mark them on your quilt top, referring to "Marking Quilting Designs" on page 28.

2. Referring to "Batting Options," "Backings," and "Layering and Basting" on page 29, layer and baste the quilt sandwich to prepare it for hand quilting.

3. Quilt the marked designs by hand, referring to "Hand Quilting" on page 30.

4. Referring to "Binding a Quilt" on page 31, bind the edges of the quilt.

5. Referring to "Finishing Touches" on page 33, add a hanging sleeve and a label to the back side of the quilt.

Rachel Thomas Pellman, 2000, Lancaster, Pennsylvania, 43" x 43".
Quilted by Sadie B. Smoker.

◆

The beauty of the Bars pattern is in its simplicity. Done here in only three colors, this pattern sometimes featured various hues in the bars and contrasting borders. The inner border of this quilt includes the grapes and grape leaves quilting design. As one Amish woman said to me, "Most anyone can quilt a straight line. It takes a good quilter to quilt a perfect circle." The tiny, perfectly quilted grapes in this example give truth to her statement.

May 20, 1950

"Grandmother always was as energetic as a house wren. She worked, even under a terrible handicap, at making quilts and knitting, so naturally it is hard for her to become resigned to the recent days in a darkened room. She can stand very little light, as she suffers with eye trouble due to a vitamin deficiency."

—From the *Budget*

FABRICS AND SUPPLIES

(fabric 42" wide after prewashing)

- ⅝ yd. burgundy solid for bars, inner border, and outer border
- 1 yd. gray-green solid for bars and outer border
- ⅞ yd. dark green solid for inner border and binding
- 2¾ yds. fabric for backing
- 47" x 47" piece of batting

CUTTING LIST

All cutting measurements include ¼" seam allowances.

From the burgundy solid, cut:

- 4 strips, each 4¼" x 26¾", for bars
- 4 squares, each 2½" x 2½", for inner border
- 4 squares, each 6¾" x 6¾", for outer border

From the gray-green solid, cut:

- 3 strips on the lengthwise grain, each 4¼" x 26¾", for bars
- 4 strips on the lengthwise grain, each 6¾" x 30¾", for outer border

From the dark green solid, cut:

- 4 strips on the lengthwise grain, each 2½" x 26¾", for inner border
- 8 strips on the lengthwise grain, each 3¾" x 28", for binding

ASSEMBLING THE QUILT TOP

1. Beginning with the burgundy strips, sew the 4¼" x 26¾" burgundy and gray-green bar strips together, alternating colors.

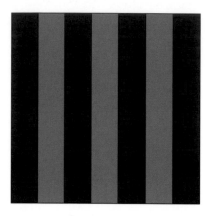

2. Sew a 2½" x 26¾" dark green inner-border strip to the top and bottom edges of the bars unit from step 1.

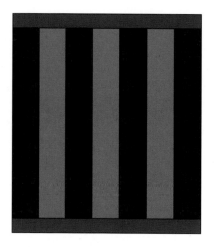

3. Sew a 2½" x 2½" burgundy square to each end of the remaining two 2½" x 26¾" dark green inner-border strips.

4. Sew an inner-border unit from step 3 to each side of the bars unit.

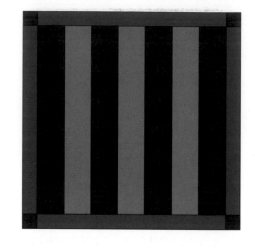

5. Sew a 6¾" x 30¾" gray-green outer-border strip to the top and bottom edges of the unit.

6. Sew a 6¾" x 6¾" burgundy square to each end of the remaining two 6¾" x 30¾" gray-green outer-border strips.

7. Sew the outer-border units from step 6 to each side of the bars unit.

QUILTING AND FINISHING

1. Select the quilting designs from pages 108–127 that you wish to use in your quilt and mark them on your quilt top, referring to "Marking Quilting Designs" on page 28.

2. Referring to "Batting Options," "Backings," and "Layering and Basting" on page 29, layer and baste the quilt sandwich to prepare it for hand quilting.

3. Quilt the marked designs by hand, referring to "Hand Quilting" on page 30.

4. Referring to "Binding a Quilt" on page 31, bind the edges of the quilt.

5. Referring to "Finishing Touches" on page 33, add a hanging sleeve and a label to the back side of the quilt.

Playmates are abundant in Amish circles. Large families provide lots of sisters, brothers, and cousins. Farms offer many opportunities for creative play.

DOUBLE NINE PATCH

Rachel Thomas Pellman, 2000, Lancaster, Pennsylvania, 42" x 42".
Quilted by Elaine W. Good.

◆

The small nine-patch units in this Double Nine Patch pattern are a great place to use your leftover scraps of fabric. Here, a wide variety of colors makes the small nine-patch units sparkle against the more subdued dark red in the small plain squares. Together, these small pieced blocks and plain squares form larger Double Nine Patch blocks.

December 1, 1932

"Last Friday about fifty menfolks gathered at the home of Sol Ropp and helped him shuck corn. They shucked 2000 bushels. There were about thirty-four women there and [they] assisted Mrs. Ropp in cooking, quilting and sewing."

—From the book *I Read It in the Budget* by Elmer S. Yoder

FABRICS AND SUPPLIES

(fabric 42" wide after prewashing)

- 20 colorful solid fabrics, each measuring 5" x 7", for Double Nine Patch blocks
- ⅔ yd. purple solid for center block, side setting and corner triangles, inner border, and outer border
- ⅞ yd. brick red solid for Double Nine Patch blocks and outer border
- ⅞ yd. dark green solid for inner border and binding
- 2¾ yds. fabric for backing
- 46" x 46" piece of batting

CUTTING LIST

All cutting measurements include ¼" seam allowances.

From the purple solid, cut:

- 1 square, 9½" x 9½", for center block
- 1 square, 14" x 14". Cut this square diagonally in both directions to form 4 side setting triangles.
- 2 squares, each 7¼" x 7¼". Cut each of these squares in half diagonally to form 4 corner triangles.
- 4 squares, each 2½" x 2½", for inner border
- 4 squares, each 6¾" x 6¾", for outer border

From the brick red solid, cut:

- 16 squares, each 3½" x 3½", for Double Nine Patch blocks
- 4 strips, each 6¾" x 30", for outer border

From the dark green solid, cut:

- 4 strips on the lengthwise grain, each 2½" x 26", for inner border
- 8 strips on the lengthwise grain, each 3¾" x 28", for binding

PIECING THE DOUBLE NINE PATCH BLOCKS

1. Divide the twenty 5" x 7" pieces of colorful solid fabric into pairs; each pair should contain contrasting values to enhance the checkerboard effect of the nine-patch units.

2. Cut the first fabric of *each* pair into 2 strips that measure 1½" x 7" and 1 strip that measures 1½" x 4".

3. Cut the second fabric of *each* pair into 1 strip that measures 1½" x 7" and 2 strips that measure 1½" x 4".

4. Sew together the three 1½" x 7" strips cut from the first pair of solid fabrics. Arrange the strips so that the 2 outer strips are the same color. Press the seam allowances toward the center strip.

5. Still working with the first pair of fabrics, sew together the three 1½" x 4" strips. Arrange the colors in reversed positions from the strip set made in step 4. Press the seam allowances toward the outer strips.

6. Cut the longer strip set into 4 segments, each 1½" wide.

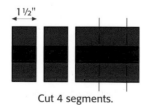

Cut 4 segments.

7. Cut the shorter strip set into 2 segments, each 1½" wide.

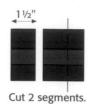

1½"

Cut 2 segments.

8. Sew together 2 segments with the contrasting color on the outside, and one segment with the contrasting color on the inside, to create a nine-patch unit. Repeat to make a second nine-patch unit in the same colors.

9. Repeat steps 4 through 8 for the remaining 9 pairs of fabric to create a total of 20 nine-patch units.

10. Sew the nine-patch units and the 3½" x 3½" brick red squares together to create the Double Nine Patch blocks. Press the seam allowances toward the brick red squares.

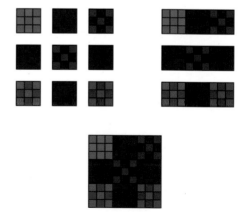

ASSEMBLING THE QUILT TOP

1. Sew 2 Double Nine Patch blocks to the 9½" x 9½" purple square, and add a purple corner triangle at each end to create the center row. To create the rows on either side, sew 2 purple side setting triangles to a Double Nine Patch block. Sew these 3 rows together and add 2 purple corner triangles to complete the quilt center.

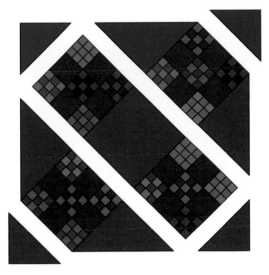

2. Sew a 2½" x 26" dark green inner-border strip to the top and bottom edges of the quilt center.

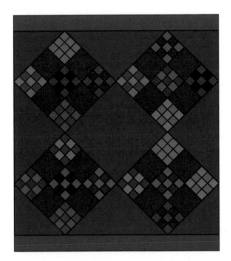

Amish farms sometimes sell bumper crops to farm markets or to the public from produce stands set up at individual farms. Young children are incorporated into the daily work routines.

3. Sew a 2½" x 2½" purple square to each end of the remaining two 2½" x 26" dark green inner-border strips.

4. Sew an inner-border unit from step 3 to each side of the quilt center.

5. Sew a 6¾" x 30" brick red outer-border strip to the top and bottom edges of the quilt center.

Surrounded by fields and meadows, Amish farms seem quiet and serene.

6. Sew a 6¾" x 6¾" purple square to each end of the remaining two 6¾" x 30" brick red outer-border strips.

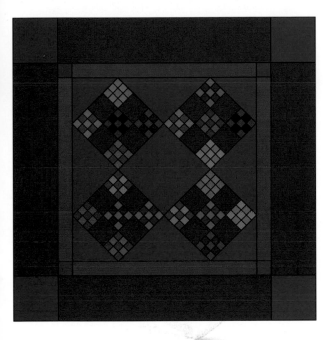

7. Sew an outer-border unit from step 6 to each side of the quilt center to complete the quilt top.

QUILTING AND FINISHING

1. Select the quilting designs from pages 108–127 that you wish to use in your quilt and mark them on your quilt top, referring to "Marking Quilting Designs" on page 28.

2. Referring to "Batting Options," "Backings," and "Layering and Basting" on page 29, layer and baste the quilt sandwich to prepare it for hand quilting.

3. Quilt the marked designs by hand, referring to "Hand Quilting" on page 30.

4. Referring to "Binding a Quilt" on page 31, bind the edges of the quilt.

5. Referring to "Finishing Touches" on page 33, add a hanging sleeve and a label to the back side of the quilt.

SUNSHINE AND SHADOW

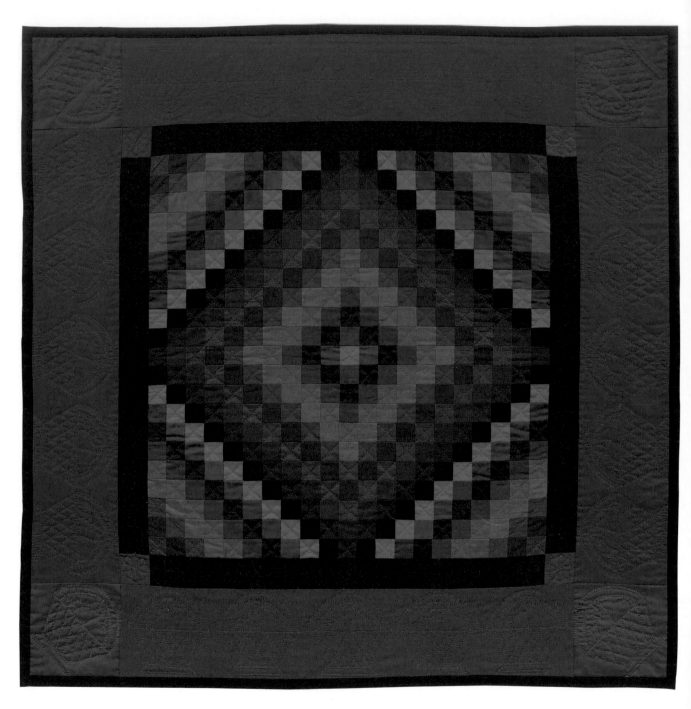

Rachel Thomas Pellman, 2000, Lancaster, Pennsylvania, 43" x 43".
Quilted by Naomi Yoder.

◆

Lancaster County Amish women used the Sunshine and Shadow pattern often, and with great success.
It was most frequently made in several colors that moved from light to dark, set against each other to form
expanding bands of deep, rich shades. It is also effective in bright, playful hues.

March 8, 1928

"The work among the women is sewing and quilting and also keeping the household things straight, while the men are butchering, making wood, and doing chores."

— From the book *I Read It in the Budget* by Elmer S. Yoder

FABRICS AND SUPPLIES

(fabric 42" wide after prewashing)

- ⅞ yd. blue solid for outer border
- ⅞ yd. burgundy solid for inner border and binding
- ¼ yd. green solid for inner border and outer border
- ⅛ yd. each of 12 different solid-colored fabrics for Sunshine and Shadow squares

   (Note: To achieve an effect similar to the quilt shown, use 3 different shades of 4 fabrics. If you use the blue, burgundy, and green solid fabrics for the squares, you will need only 9 additional fabrics.)
- 2¾ yds. fabric for backing
- 47" x 47" piece of batting

CUTTING LIST

All cutting measurements include ¼" seam allowances.

From the assorted 12 solid-colored fabrics, cut:

- Fabric #1—37 squares, each 1¾" x 1¾"
- Fabric #2—36 squares, each 1¾" x 1¾"
- Fabric #3—36 squares, each 1¾" x 1¾"
- Fabric #4—36 squares, each 1¾" x 1¾"
- Fabric #5—36 squares, each 1¾" x 1¾"
- Fabric #6—36 squares, each 1¾" x 1¾"
- Fabric #7—36 squares, each 1¾" x 1¾"
- Fabric #8—36 squares, each 1¾" x 1¾"
- Fabric #9—36 squares, each 1¾" x 1¾"
- Fabric #10—36 squares, each 1¾" x 1¾"
- Fabric #11—40 squares, each 1¾" x 1¾"
- Fabric #12—40 squares, each 1¾" x 1¾"

From the blue solid, cut:

- 4 strips on the lengthwise grain, each 6¾" x 30¾", for outer border

From the burgundy solid, cut:

- 4 strips on the lengthwise grain, each 2½" x 26¾", for inner border
- 8 strips, each 3¾" x 28", for binding

From the green solid, cut:

- 4 squares, each 2½" x 2½", for inner border
- 4 squares, each 6¾" x 6¾", for outer border

ASSEMBLING THE QUILT TOP

1. Using the numbered diagram as a guide, begin sewing the assorted solid-colored 1¾" x 1¾" squares into rows.

9	8	7	6	5	4	3	2	1	12	11	12	1	2	3	4	5	6	7	8	9

8	7	6	5	4	3	2	1	12	11	10	11	12	1	2	3	4	5	6	7	8

2. Sew the rows of squares together to complete the Sunshine and Shadow pattern for the quilt center.

9	8	7	6	5	4	3	2	1	12	11	12	1	2	3	4	5	6	7	8	9
8	7	6	5	4	3	2	1	12	11	10	11	12	1	2	3	4	5	6	7	8
7	6	5	4	3	2	1	12	11	10	9	10	11	12	1	2	3	4	5	6	7
6	5	4	3	2	1	12	11	10	9	8	9	10	11	12	1	2	3	4	5	6
5	4	3	2	1	12	11	10	9	8	7	8	9	10	11	12	1	2	3	4	5
4	3	2	1	12	11	10	9	8	7	6	7	8	9	10	11	12	1	2	3	4
3	2	1	12	11	10	9	8	7	6	5	6	7	8	9	10	11	12	1	2	3
2	1	12	11	10	9	8	7	6	5	4	5	6	7	8	9	10	11	12	1	2
1	12	11	10	9	8	7	6	5	4	3	4	5	6	7	8	9	10	11	12	1
12	11	10	9	8	7	6	5	4	3	2	3	4	5	6	7	8	9	10	11	12
11	10	9	8	7	6	5	4	3	2	1	2	3	4	5	6	7	8	9	10	11
12	11	10	9	8	7	6	5	4	3	2	3	4	5	6	7	8	9	10	11	12
1	12	11	10	9	8	7	6	5	4	3	4	5	6	7	8	9	10	11	12	1
2	1	12	11	10	9	8	7	6	5	4	5	6	7	8	9	10	11	12	1	2
3	2	1	12	11	10	9	8	7	6	5	6	7	8	9	10	11	12	1	2	3
4	3	2	1	12	11	10	9	8	7	6	7	8	9	10	11	12	1	2	3	4
5	4	3	2	1	12	11	10	9	8	7	8	9	10	11	12	1	2	3	4	5
6	5	4	3	2	1	12	11	10	9	8	9	10	11	12	1	2	3	4	5	6
7	6	5	4	3	2	1	12	11	10	9	10	11	12	1	2	3	4	5	6	7
8	7	6	5	4	3	2	1	12	11	10	11	12	1	2	3	4	5	6	7	8
9	8	7	6	5	4	3	2	1	12	11	12	1	2	3	4	5	6	7	8	9

3. Sew a 2½" x 26¾" burgundy inner-border strip to the top and bottom edges of the quilt center.

4. Sew a 2½" x 2½" green square to each end of the remaining two 2½" x 26¾" burgundy inner-border strips.

5. Sew an inner-border unit from step 4 to each side of the quilt center.

6. Sew a 6¾" x 30¾" blue outer-border strip to the top and bottom edges of the quilt center.

7. Sew a 6¾" x 6¾" green square to each end of the remaining two 6¾" x 30¾" blue outer-border strips.

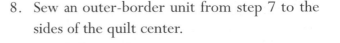

8. Sew an outer-border unit from step 7 to the sides of the quilt center.

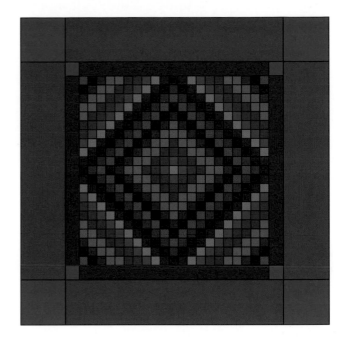

QUILTING AND FINISHING

1. Select the quilting designs from pages 108–127 that you wish to use in your quilt and mark them on your quilt top, referring to "Marking Quilting Designs" on page 28.

2. Referring to "Batting Options," "Backings," and "Layering and Basting" on page 29, layer and baste the quilt sandwich to prepare it for hand quilting.

3. Quilt the marked designs by hand, referring to "Hand Quilting" on page 30.

4. Referring to "Binding a Quilt" on page 31, bind the edges of the quilt.

5. Referring to "Finishing Touches" on page 33, add a hanging sleeve and a label to the back side of the quilt.

TRIPLE IRISH CHAIN

Rachel Thomas Pellman, 2000, Lancaster, Pennsylvania, 43" x 43".
Quilted by Sadie B. Smoker.

◆

Two contrasting colors create the Irish Chain effect in this pattern, and its angular lines are enhanced by simple, straight lines quilted diagonally through the squares. The open spaces between the pieced blocks provide a canvas for gracefully quilted feathered circles.

August 5, 1954

"A rather unusual quilting was held at John King's near Bird-in-Hand on Saturday in honor of their twin girls, Mary and Mattie. Five pairs of twin girls were invited."

—From the book *I Read It in the Budget* by Elmer S. Yoder

FABRICS AND SUPPLIES

(fabric 42" wide after prewashing)

♦ 1¼ yds. dark green solid for inner border, Blocks I and II, and binding

♦ ⅝ yd. gray solid for Blocks I and II, inner border, and outer border

♦ 1⅛ yds. burgundy solid for outer border and Blocks I and II

♦ 2¾ yds. fabric for backing

♦ 47" x 47" piece of batting

CUTTING LIST

All cutting measurements include ¼" seam allowances.

From the dark green solid, cut:

♦ 4 strips on the lengthwise grain, each 2½" x 26¾", for inner border

♦ 116 squares, each 1¾" x 1¾", for Blocks I and II

♦ 8 strips on the lengthwise grain, each 3¾" x 28", for binding

From the gray solid, cut:

♦ 4 squares, each 6¾" x 6¾", for outer border

♦ 4 squares, each 2½" x 2½", for inner border

♦ 4 pieces, each 4¼" x 9¼", for Block II

♦ 8 pieces, each 3" x 4¼", for Block II

♦ 36 squares, each 1¾" x 1¾", for Blocks I and II

From the burgundy solid, cut:

♦ 4 strips on the lengthwise grain, each 6¾" x 30¾", for outer border

♦ 157 squares, each 1¾" x 1¾", for Blocks I and II

PIECING BLOCK I

1. Referring to the Block I diagram below, sew together 1¾" x 1¾" dark green, gray, and burgundy squares to form 7 rows. Press all seams in each row in the same direction.

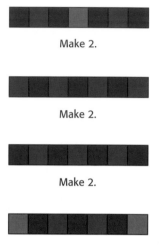

Make 2.

Make 2.

Make 2.

Make 1.

2. Sew the 7 rows of Block I together, with the seam allowances facing in opposite directions so that the seams will match easily.

Block I
Make 5.

3. Repeat steps 1 and 2 to make a total of 5 of Block I.

Largely untouched by the modern world, Amish families live surrounded by the natural beauty of their farmland.

PIECING BLOCK II

1. Sew together 1 dark green, 1 gray, and 2 burgundy 1¾" x 1¾" squares as shown, forming a four-patch unit. Make a total of 16 of these four-patch units.

Make 16.

2. Sew a four-patch unit to each end of a 3" x 4¼" gray piece, making sure that the colors in the four-patch units are positioned as shown. Make a total of 8 of these units.

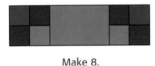

Make 8.

3. Sew together 2 units from step 2 and one 4¼" x 9¼" gray piece, completing Block II. Make a total of 4 of Block II.

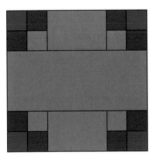

Block II
Make 4.

ASSEMBLING THE QUILT TOP

1. Sew Blocks I and II together into 3 rows, referring to the diagram for placement. Sew the 3 rows together to complete the quilt center.

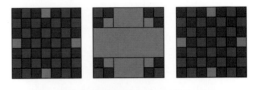

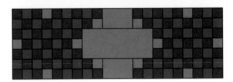

2. Sew a 2½" x 26¾" dark green inner-border strip to the top and bottom edges of the quilt center.

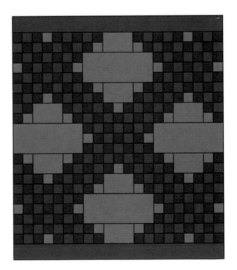

*Sunset signals the end of the workday. Long summer days accommodate the extended hours
required to store foods from gardens and fields for winter consumption by family and farm animals.*

3. Sew a 2½" x 2½" gray square to each end of
   the remaining 2 dark green inner-border strips.

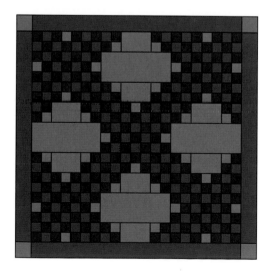

4. Sew an inner-border unit from step 3 to each
   side of the quilt center.

5. Sew a 6¾" x 30¾" burgundy outer-border
   strip to the top and bottom edges.

6. Sew a 6¾" x 6¾" gray square to each end of the remaining 2 outer-border strips.

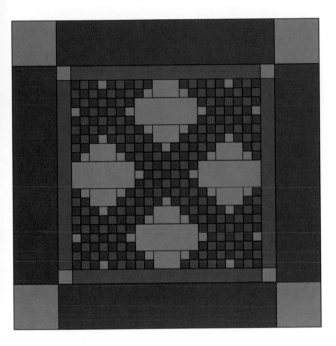

7. Sew an outer-border unit from step 6 to each side of the quilt center, completing the quilt top.

QUILTING AND FINISHING

1. Select the quilting designs from pages 108–127 that you wish to use in your quilt and mark them on your quilt top, referring to "Marking Quilting Designs" on page 28.

2. Referring to "Batting Options," "Backings," and "Layering and Basting" on page 29, layer and baste the quilt sandwich to prepare it for hand quilting.

3. Quilt the marked designs by hand, referring to "Hand Quilting" on page 30.

4. Referring to "Binding a Quilt" on page 31, bind the edges of the quilt.

5. Referring to "Finishing Touches" on page 33, add a hanging sleeve and a label to the back side of the quilt.

LONE STAR

Rachel Thomas Pellman, 2000, Lancaster, Pennsylvania, 43" x 43".
Quilted by Sadie B. Smoker.

———◆———

Exploding with color, this dramatic Lone Star pattern was a perennial favorite with Amish quiltmakers in both Lancaster County and the Midwest. This quilt shows a color scheme that was typical of Lancaster County, with deep, rich purples, reds, and greens. Midwestern Lone Stars tended to feature a wider range of colors, often incorporating yellows and golds.

January 14, 1926

"There was a wood chopping and a quilting at Andy Byler's on New Year's Day and also an oyster supper in the evening."

—From the book *I Read It in the Budget* by Elmer S. Yoder

FABRICS AND SUPPLIES

(fabric 42" wide after prewashing)

- 1¼ yds. burgundy solid for diamonds and border
- ⅛ yd. brick red solid for diamonds
- ¼ yd. medium green solid for diamonds
- ¼ yd. dark green solid for diamonds
- ⅜ yd. medium purple for diamonds
- 1⅜ yds. dark purple solid for diamonds, plain blocks, side setting triangles, and binding
- 2¾ yds. fabric for backing
- 47" x 47" piece of batting

CUTTING LIST

All cutting measurements include ¼" seam allowances.

From the burgundy solid, cut:

- 1 strip, 1½" x 42", for diamonds
- 2 strips on the lengthwise grain, each 6¾" x 30", for border
- 2 strips on the lengthwise grain, each 6¾" x 42¾", for border

From the brick red solid, cut:

- 2 strips, each 1½" x 42", for diamonds

From the medium green solid, cut:

- 3 strips, each 1½" x 42", for diamonds

From the dark green solid, cut:

- 4 strips, each 1½" x 42", for diamonds

From the medium purple solid, cut:

- 5 strips, each 1½" x 42", for diamonds

From the dark purple solid, cut:

- 3 strips, each 1½" x 42", for diamonds
- 4 squares, each 9¼" x 9¼", for plain blocks
- 1 square, 13½" x 13½". Cut this square diagonally in both directions to create 4 side setting triangles.
- 8 strips, each 3¾" x 28", for binding

Piecing the Lone Star

1. Sew together six 1½" x 42" strips in the following color sequence: burgundy, brick red,
   medium green, dark green, medium purple,
   and dark purple. As you add each strip, offset
   it 1" from the end of the previous strip so that
   the strips are staggered. Carefully press all of
   the seam allowances in one direction and
   avoid stretching or distorting the strips.

2. Align the 45° line on an acrylic ruler with one
   of the seams, and rotary cut the strip set into
   1½"-wide segments. Cut a total of 16 of these
   segments.

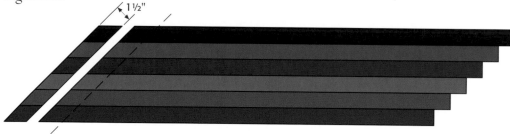

3. Referring to steps 1 and 2, sew together a second strip set consisting of six 1½" x 42" strips
   in the following color sequence: brick red,
   medium green, dark green, medium purple,
   dark purple, medium purple. Carefully press
   all of the seam allowances in one direction,
   and avoid stretching or distorting the strips.

4. Align the 45° line on an acrylic ruler with one of the seams, and rotary cut the strip set into 1½"-wide segments. Cut a total of 16 of these segments.

5. In the same manner, sew together a third strip set consisting of 1½" x 42" strips in the following color sequence: medium green, dark green, medium purple, dark purple, medium purple, dark green. Carefully press all of the seam allowances in one direction, and avoid stretching or distorting the strips.

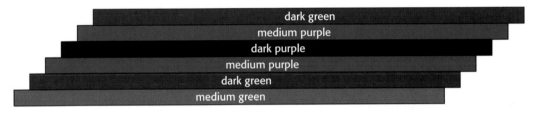

6. Align the 45° line on an acrylic ruler with one of the seams, and rotary cut the strip set into 1½"-wide segments. Cut a total of 16 segments from this strip set.

7. Sew together 6 diamond segments as shown for each star point. Make a total of 6 identical Lone Star points.

8. Sew 2 Lone Star points together, leaving ¼" free at the end of the seam so you can set in the plain blocks and side setting triangles later. Repeat to make 3 more pairs of Lone Star points.

Stop stitching ¼" from outer edge.

Make 4.

9. Sew 2 pairs of Lone Star points together to create half of the Lone Star, leaving ¼" free at the end of the seam as before.

Stop stitching ¼" from outer edge.

10. Sew the 2 halves of the Lone Star together, leaving ¼" free at each end of the seam.

ASSEMBLING THE QUILT TOP

1. To set in the four 9¼" x 9¼" dark purple plain blocks at the corners of the Lone Star, start by marking a small dot on the wrong side of each dark purple plain block to indicate the inner corner of the ¼" seam allowance. With the dark purple plain block on top, match the marked dot to the inner corner of the Lone Star point and pin in place. Sew inward from the outer tip of the first Lone Star point, stopping when you reach the inner corner of the Lone Star point. Pivot and sew the next side of the dark purple plain block to the next Lone Star point, stopping when you reach the outer tip of the Lone Star point. Press the seam allowance toward the Lone Star point. Repeat this step to set in the remaining 3 dark purple plain blocks.

Set squares and triangles into Lone Star points matching the ¼" opening on the Lone Star points with the corner of the ¼" seam allowance marked by a dot on the squares and triangles.

2. Referring to step 1, set in the dark purple side setting triangles in the same manner. Then trim away any excess fabric from the outer edges, making sure to leave a ¼" seam allowance beyond all of the Lone Star points.

3. Sew a 6¾" x 30" burgundy border strip to the top and bottom edges of the Lone Star. Press the seam allowances toward the border strips and trim the borders even with the edges of the quilt top.

4. Sew the two 6¾" x 42¾" burgundy border strips to the sides of the quilt top. Trim the border strips even with the quilt top. Press the seam allowances toward the border strips.

QUILTING AND FINISHING

1. Select the quilting designs from pages 108–127 that you wish to use in your quilt and mark them on your quilt top, referring to "Marking Quilting Designs" on page 28.

2. Referring to "Batting Options," "Backings," and "Layering and Basting" on page 29, layer and baste the quilt sandwich to prepare it for hand quilting.

3. Quilt the marked designs by hand, referring to "Hand Quilting" on page 30.

4. Referring to "Binding a Quilt" on page 31, bind the edges of the quilt.

5. Referring to "Finishing Touches" on page 33 add a hanging sleeve and a label to the back side of the quilt.

MIDWESTERN QUILTS

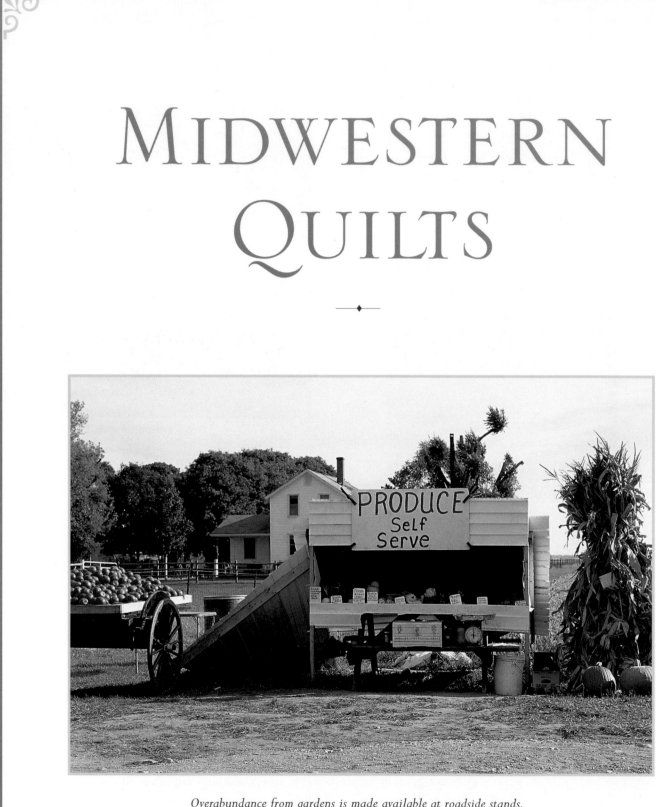

Overabundance from gardens is made available at roadside stands.
Preserved fruits, jellies, and home-baked goodies are also sold.

OCEAN WAVES

BEAR'S PAW

BASKETS

OHIO STAR

MONKEY WRENCH

SHOOFLY

Rachel Thomas Pellman, 2000, Lancaster, Pennsylvania, 37" x 37".
Quilted by Carol Oberholtzer.

♦

A multitude of colors adds visual dimension to this Ocean Waves pattern. Though it was most often made in Amish communities in landlocked midwestern states, the array of different blues creates a feeling of movement and current that is reminiscent of the ocean. The fan quilting in the outer border adds an illusion of rolling waves.

October 21, 1950

"Mrs. Lizzie Miller from Dakota is at the home of her brother, Dan Coblentz, and is making carpets by hand for others. Mrs. Dan Coblentz is piecing quilts. My mother is also piecing quilts when she feels able to do so."

—From the *Budget*

FABRICS AND SUPPLIES

(fabric 42" wide after prewashing)

♦ 9" x 12" scraps of 13 to 20 different solid-colored fabrics for Ocean Waves blocks

♦ ⅞ yd. khaki solid for outer border and Ocean Waves blocks

♦ ⅝ yd. burgundy solid for inner border and binding

♦ 1¼ yds. fabric for backing

♦ 41" x 41" piece of batting

If you wish, you can use more than 20 solid-colored scrap fabrics for the Ocean Waves blocks. The greater your variety of colors, the more visually interesting the quilt pattern will be. More fabrics will also decrease the chances of the same fabrics occurring side by side when you assemble the blocks.

CUTTING LIST

All cutting measurements include ¼" seam allowances.

From the 9" x 12" scraps, cut:

♦ 192 squares, each 2⅜" x 2⅜", for Ocean Waves blocks

From the khaki solid, cut:

♦ 2 strips, each 5" x 28½", for outer border

♦ 2 strips, each 5" x 37½", for outer border

♦ 32 squares, each 2⅜" x 2⅜", for Ocean Waves blocks

♦ 32 squares, each 2" x 2", for Ocean Waves blocks

From the burgundy solid, cut:

♦ 2 strips, each 2½" x 24½", for inner border

♦ 2 strips, each 2½" x 28½", for inner border

♦ 4 strips, each 2½" x 42", for binding

Note: This midwestern pattern was often rectangular in antique Amish quilts. As a small wall quilt, however, it seems more appropriate as a square, with a symmetrical pattern of Ocean Waves blocks.

PIECING THE OCEAN WAVES BLOCKS

NOTE: *Each Ocean Waves block features same-color triangles and a square at 2 opposite corners of the block. These will create the background areas between the pieced triangles when the blocks are set side-by-side.*

1. Place 160 of the 2⅜" x 2⅜" squares of scrap fabrics together in randomly colored pairs, with right sides together. Rotary cut the squares diagonally from corner to corner. Sew each of these triangle pairs together along the diagonal edges, taking care not to stretch the fabric. Press the seam allowances to one side and trim away the excess points at the end of each seam.

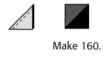

Make 160.

2. To make the 64 triangle-square units for the corners of the Ocean Waves blocks, pair the thirty-two 2⅜" x 2⅜" khaki squares with the remaining thirty-two 2⅜" x 2⅜" squares cut from the 9" x 12" scraps. Cut each pair of squares diagonally from corner to corner to create 2 triangle pairs. Sew these paired triangles together along the diagonal edges, taking care not to stretch the fabric. Press the seam allowances to one side and trim away the excess points at the end of each seam as in step 1.

Make 64.

3. Referring to the illustration below, sew a 2" x 2" khaki square to a triangle-square unit that contains a khaki triangle. Add 2 more randomly colored triangle-square units, making sure that the diagonal seams slant in the same direction.

NOTE: *Only use triangle-square units that have khaki fabric at 2 opposite corners of the Ocean Waves blocks.*

4. Referring to the illustration below, sew row 2 of the Ocean Waves block, beginning with a khaki triangle-square unit, followed by 3 more randomly colored triangle-square units.

5. Referring to the illustration below, sew rows 3 and 4.

NOTE: *The color placements in these rows are the reverse of rows 1 and 2.*

6. Sew rows 1 through 4 together to create the Ocean Waves block. Repeat steps 3 through 6 to piece a total of 16 Ocean Waves blocks.

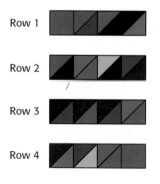

Row 1
Row 2
Row 3
Row 4

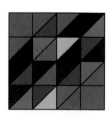

Ocean Waves block diagram

ASSEMBLING THE QUILT TOP

1. Sew a row of 4 Ocean Waves blocks, alternating the position of the blocks. Make a total of 4 of these rows.

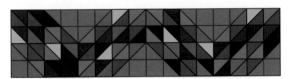

2. Join the 4 rows of Ocean Waves blocks.

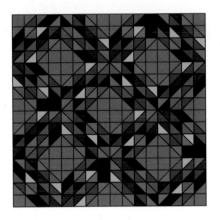

3. Sew the 2½" x 24½" burgundy inner-border strips to the top and bottom edges of the quilt center. Trim the border strips even with the quilt center. Sew the 2½" x 28½" burgundy inner-border strips to the sides.

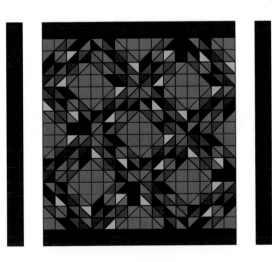

4. Sew the 5" x 28½" khaki outer-border strips to the top and bottom edges of the quilt center. Trim the border strips even with the quilt center. Sew the 5" x 37½" outer-border strips to the sides of the quilt center, completing the quilt top.

QUILTING AND FINISHING

1. Select the quilting designs from pages 108–127 that you wish to use in your quilt and mark them on your quilt top, referring to "Marking Quilting Designs" on page 28.

2. Referring to "Batting Options," "Backings," and "Layering and Basting" on page 29, layer and baste the quilt sandwich to prepare it for hand quilting.

3. Quilt the marked designs by hand, referring to "Hand Quilting" on page 30.

4. Referring to "Binding a Quilt" on page 31, bind the edges of the quilt.

5. Referring to "Finishing Touches" on page 33, add a hanging sleeve and a label to the back side of the quilt.

BEAR'S PAW

Rachel Thomas Pellman, 2001, Lancaster, Pennsylvania, 35" x 46".
Quilted by Sadie B. Smoker.

Black was used often by Amish quiltmakers in the Midwest to create a most dramatic background for pieced blocks, as in this classic Bear's Paw pattern. Simple, straight line quilting adds a subtle design element without detracting from the precisely pieced Bear's Paw blocks.

January 29, 1951

"On Tuesday, Mrs. Ezra L. Bontrager had a quilting. Ezra's brothers and sisters were there to help. On Wednesday she had her married children, [myself], and mother to help finish it."

—From the *Budget*

FABRICS AND SUPPLIES

(fabric 42" wide after prewashing)

- 1 yd. red solid for Bear's Paw blocks, inner border, and binding
- 1⅜ yds. black solid for outer border, Bear's Paw blocks, plain blocks, and side setting and corner triangles
- 1⅜ yds. fabric for backing
- 39" x 50" piece of batting

CUTTING LIST

All cutting measurements include ¼" seam allowances.

From the red solid, cut:

- 2 strips, each 2½" x 23¼", for inner border
- 2 strips, each 2½" x 38½", for inner border
- 2 strips, each 2½" x 38", for binding
- 4 strips, each 2½" x 26", for binding
- 48 squares, each 2" x 2", for Bear's Paw blocks

- 24 squares, each 2¾" x 2¾", for Bear's Paw blocks
- 6 squares, each 1⅝" x 1⅝", for Bear's Paw blocks

From the black solid, cut:

- 2 strips on the lengthwise grain, each 4½" x 27¼", for outer border
- 2 strips on the lengthwise grain, each 4½" x 46½", for outer border
- 24 rectangles, each 1⅝" x 3⅞", for Bear's Paw blocks
- 24 squares, each 1⅝" x 1⅝", for Bear's Paw blocks
- 48 squares, each 2" x 2", for Bear's Paw blocks
- 2 squares, each 8⅜" x 8⅜", for plain blocks
- 2 squares, each 12½" x 12½". Cut each square diagonally from corner to corner in both directions to form 8 side setting triangles. There will be 2 triangles left over.
  Note: This cutting method places the grainline of the side setting triangles at the edges of the quilt center.
- 2 squares, each 6½" x 6½". Cut each square diagonally from corner to corner to form 4 corner triangles.

PIECING THE BEAR'S PAW BLOCKS

1. Pair a 2" x 2" red square with a 2" x 2" black square, right sides together. Rotary cut the squares diagonally from corner to corner, creating 2 triangle pairs. Sew the triangle pairs together along the diagonal edge, taking care not to stretch the fabric. Press the seam allowances toward the lighter fabric, and trim away the points at the ends of the seams. Repeat to form 96 triangle-square units.

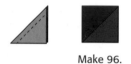

Make 96.

2. Referring to the diagram, sew together 2 triangle-square units. Sew this row of triangle-square units to a 2¾" x 2¾" red square as shown. Sew a row of 2 triangle-square units and one 1⅝" x 1⅝" black square together as shown. Sew this row to the red-square/triangle-square unit, completing the "bear's paw." Repeat to make a total of 24 bear's paw units.

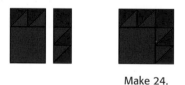

Make 24.

3. Sew a bear's paw unit to each side of a 1⅝" x 3⅞" black rectangle. Make a total of 12 of these units.

Make 12.

4. Sew a 1⅝" x 3⅞" black rectangle to each side of a 1⅝" x 1⅝" red square. Make 6 of these rectangle units.

Make 6.

5. Sew a bear's paw unit from step 3 to each side of the rectangle unit from step 4, completing a Bear's Paw block. Make a total of 6 Bear's Paw blocks.

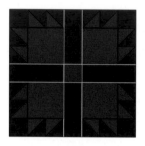

Make 6.

ASSEMBLING THE QUILT TOP

1. Refer to the diagram to sew the Bear's Paw blocks, the 8⅜" x 8⅜" black plain blocks, and

the black side setting and corner triangles into 4 rows. Sew the rows together to complete the quilt center.

NOTE: *The side setting and corner triangles are slightly larger than necessary. To attach the side setting triangles, align the inside point of each side setting triangle with the edge of the adjacent Bear's Paw block. Trim the side setting triangles even with the quilt center after all of the rows are joined. To attach the corner triangles, align the center of the adjacent Bear's Paw block with the center of the corner triangle. Trim away the excess fabric from the corner triangles after the quilt center is completely assembled.*

2. Sew the 2½" x 23¼" red inner-border strips to the top and bottom edges of the quilt center. Sew the two 2½" x 38½" red inner-border strips to the sides of the quilt center.

3. Sew the 4½" x 27¼" black outer-border strips to the top and bottom edges of the quilt center. Sew the two 4½" x 46½" black outer-border strips to the sides of the quilt center.

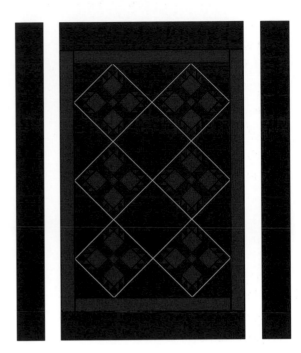

QUILTING AND FINISHING

1. Select the quilting designs from pages 108–127 that you wish to use in your quilt and mark them on your quilt top, referring to "Marking Quilting Designs" on page 28.

2. Referring to "Batting Options," "Backings," and "Layering and Basting" on page 29, layer and baste the quilt sandwich to prepare it for hand quilting.

3. Quilt the marked designs by hand, referring to "Hand Quilting" on page 30.

4. Referring to "Binding a Quilt" on page 31, bind the edges of the quilt.

5. Referring to "Finishing Touches" on page 33, add a hanging sleeve and a label to the back side of the quilt.

BASKETS

Rachel Thomas Pellman, 2001, Lancaster, Pennsylvania, 38" x 47".
Quilted by Sadie B. Smoker.

◆

Perky pieced baskets alternate with delicately quilted feathers in this quilt. The patience required to make the Basket blocks will be rewarded by the elegant look of the finished piece. Quilted cables outline the border, adding soft curves to this angular quilt pattern. Note: This Basket pattern was also used by quiltmakers in Lancaster County. To make a Lancaster-style Basket quilt, simply decrease the number of baskets to 3 by 3 to make the quilt square, and increase the outer border width to 6¾" as in "Center Diamond" on page 36.

February 8, 1951

"I expect to put a quilt in the frame Wednesday. Whoever wishes to help quilt is cordially invited."

—From the *Budget*

FABRICS AND SUPPLIES

(fabric 42" wide after prewashing)

♦ 1⅛ yds. magenta solid for Basket blocks and binding
♦ 1⅛ yds. medium green solid for Basket blocks and inner border
♦ 1½ yds. dark green solid for plain blocks, side setting and corner triangles, and outer border
♦ 1½ yds. fabric for backing
♦ 42" x 51" piece of batting

CUTTING LIST

All cutting measurements include ¼" seam allowances.

From the magenta solid, cut:

♦ 48 squares, each 2⅛" x 2⅛", for Basket blocks
♦ 6 squares, each 4⅝" x 4⅝", for Basket blocks
♦ 2 strips, each 2½" x 42", for binding
♦ 4 strips, each 2½" x 28", for binding

From the medium green solid, cut:

♦ 48 squares, each 2⅛" x 2⅛", for Basket blocks
♦ 6 squares, each 4⅝" x 4⅝", for Basket blocks
♦ 24 rectangles, each 1¾" x 4¼", for Basket blocks
♦ 24 squares, each 1¾" x 1¾", for Basket blocks
♦ 2 strips, each 2" x 27", for inner border
♦ 2 strips, each 2" x 39", for inner border

From the dark green solid, cut:

♦ 6 squares, each 6¾" x 6¾", for plain blocks
♦ 3 squares, each 10⅛" x 10⅛". Cut each of these squares diagonally in both directions to create 6 side setting triangles. There will be 2 triangles left over.
♦ 2 squares, each 5⅜" x 5⅜". Cut each of these squares in half diagonally to create 4 corner triangles.
♦ 2 strips on the lengthwise grain, each 4½" x 30⅛", for outer border
♦ 2 strips on the lengthwise grain, each 4½" x 47", for outer border

PIECING THE BASKET BLOCKS

1. Pair the 2⅛" x 2⅛" magenta squares with the 2⅛" x 2⅛" medium green squares, right sides together. Cut these pairs of squares in half diagonally to create 96 triangle pairs. Stitch the triangles together along the diagonal edges to create 96 small triangle-square units, taking care not to stretch the fabric as you sew. Press the seams toward the lighter fabric.

Make 96.

2. Pair the 4⅝" x 4⅝" magenta squares with the 4⅝" x 4⅝" medium green squares, right sides together. Cut these pairs of squares in half diagonally to create 12 triangle pairs. Stitch the triangles together along the diagonal edges to create 12 large triangle-square units, taking care not to stretch the fabric as you sew. Press the seams toward the lighter fabric.

Make 12.

3. Sew a row of 3 small triangle-square units, referring to the diagram for color placement. Sew a row of 3 small triangle-square units and a 1¾" x 1¾" medium green square, referring to the diagram for color placement. Sew these 2 rows to a large triangle-square unit, referring to the diagram. Repeat to make a total of 12 of these units.

Make 12.

4. Sew a small triangle-square unit to a 1¾" x 4¼" medium green rectangle, referring to the diagram for color placement. Sew another 1¾" x 4¼" medium green rectangle and a small triangle-square unit together, adding a 1¾" x 1¾" medium green square at the end; refer to the diagram for color placement. Sew these strips to one of the units from step 3 to complete a Basket block. Press the seam allowances toward the lighter fabric. Repeat to make a total of 12 Basket blocks.

Make 12.

ASSEMBLING THE QUILT TOP

1. Referring to the diagram, join the Basket blocks and the 6¾" x 6¾" dark green plain blocks to form diagonal rows as shown. Add

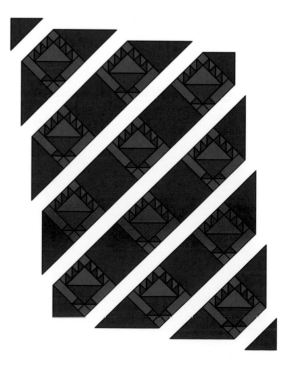

the side setting triangles, matching the right angle of the triangle to the side of the adjacent Basket block. When you add the corner triangles, align the center of the corner triangle with the center of the adjacent Basket block. Sew the rows together to complete the quilt center. Trim any excess fabric from the side setting triangles and corner triangles, making sure to allow for the ¼" seam allowance on all 4 sides of the quilt center.

2. Sew the 2" x 27" medium green inner-border strips to the top and bottom edges of the quilt center. Trim the border strips even with the quilt center. Sew the 2" x 39" medium green inner-border strips to the sides.

3. Sew the 4½" x 30⅛" dark green outer-border strips to the top and bottom edges of the quilt center. Sew the 4½" x 47" dark green outer-border strips to the sides of the quilt center, completing the Baskets quilt top.

QUILTING AND FINISHING

1. Select the quilting designs from pages 108–127 that you wish to use in your quilt and mark them on your quilt top, referring to "Marking Quilting Designs" on page 28.

2. Referring to "Batting Options," "Backings," and "Layering and Basting" on page 29, layer and baste the quilt sandwich to prepare it for hand quilting.

3. Quilt the marked designs by hand, referring to "Hand Quilting" on page 30.

4. Referring to "Binding a Quilt" on page 31, bind the edges of the quilt.

5. Referring to "Finishing Touches" on page 33, add a hanging sleeve and a label to the back side of the quilt.

OHIO STAR

Rachel Thomas Pellman, 2001, Lancaster, Pennsylvania, 38" x 46".
Quilted by Barbara A. Hershey.

Bright stars in two colors twinkle against the dark background colors in this Ohio Star quilt. Straight-line quilting runs through the Ohio Star blocks, and feathered circles fill the open spaces between the stars.

October 5, 1950

"The past week has been warm and summery again, the Golden Season of harvest. Silo filling is underway and corn is being cut, while among the women folk, the last of the summer canning is being done."

—From the *Budget*

FABRICS AND SUPPLIES

(fabric 42" wide after prewashing)
- ¼ yd. gold solid for Ohio Star blocks
- 1¼ yds. rust solid for Ohio Star blocks, inner border, and binding
- ¼ yd. tan solid for Ohio Star blocks
- 1½ yds. dark purple solid for plain blocks, side setting and corner triangles, and outer border
- 1⅜ yds. fabric for backing
- 42" x 50" piece of batting

CUTTING LIST

All cutting measurements include ¼" seam allowances.

From the gold solid, cut:
- 48 squares, each 2" x 2", for Ohio Star blocks
- 6 squares, each 3½" x 3½", for Ohio Star blocks

From the rust solid, cut:
- 2 strips, each 2½" x 26", for inner border
- 2 strips, each 2½" x 38½", for inner border
- 2 strips, each 2½" x 42", for binding
- 4 strips, each 2½" x 28", for binding
- 48 squares, each 2" x 2", for Ohio Star blocks
- 48 rectangles, each 2" x 3½", for Ohio Star blocks

From the tan solid, cut:
- 48 squares, each 2" x 2", for Ohio Star blocks
- 6 squares, each 3½" x 3½", for Ohio Star blocks

From the dark purple solid, cut:
- 2 strips on the lengthwise grain, each 4½" x 30", for outer border
- 2 strips on the lengthwise grain, each 4½" x 46½", for outer border
- 6 squares, each 6½" x 6½", for plain blocks
- 3 squares, each 10½" x 10½". Cut these squares diagonally from corner to corner in both directions to create 10 side setting triangles. There will be 2 triangles left over.
- 2 squares, each 5½" x 5½". Cut each of these squares in half diagonally to create 4 corner triangles.

PIECING THE OHIO STAR BLOCKS

1. Using a sharp pencil, draw a diagonal line from corner to corner on the *wrong side* of each of two 2" x 2" gold squares. Place a marked gold square at one end of a 2" x 3½" rust rectangle, with right sides together and the corners precisely aligned. The pencil line should go from the upper outside corner down to the center of the rectangle. Stitch exactly on this marked line.

> *When drawing the diagonal lines on the fabric, place the gold squares on a piece of fine-grit sandpaper to help prevent shifting and increase precision.*

2. Trim away the excess fabric, leaving a ¼" seam allowance as shown. Press the seam allowance toward the gold Ohio Star point.

3. Repeat steps 1 and 2 to add a gold Ohio Star point at the other end of the rust triangle.

4. Repeat steps 1 and 2 to make a total of 24 rectangular star-point units in the gold and rust combination.

> *Save the small triangles you trim away from the rectangle units, and use them for a future miniature project.*

5. Sew a gold-and-rust star-point unit to the top and bottom edges of a 3½" x 3½" gold square.

Make 1.

6. Sew a 2" x 2" rust square to each end of a gold-and-rust star-point unit. Make 2.

Make 2.

7. Sew the units from step 6 to each side of the units from step 5, completing the Ohio Star block. Repeat steps 5 and 6 to make a total of 6 Ohio Star blocks in the gold-and-rust combination.

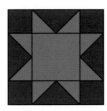

Make 6.

8. Repeat steps 1 through 7, replacing the gold pieces with tan, to make a total of 6 Ohio Star blocks in the tan-and-rust color combination.

Make 6.

Crops grown in the fields are stored in large barns and silos to feed horses and livestock through the winter months.

ASSEMBLING THE QUILT TOP

1. Referring to the diagram, join the Ohio Star blocks and the 6½" x 6½" dark purple plain blocks together to form diagonal rows as shown. Add the side setting triangles, matching the right angle of the triangle to the side of the adjacent Ohio Star block. When you add the corner triangles, align the center of the corner triangle with the center of the adjacent Ohio Star block. Sew the rows together to complete the quilt center. Trim away any excess fabric from the side setting and corner triangles, making sure to allow for the ¼" seam allowance on all 4 sides of the quilt center.

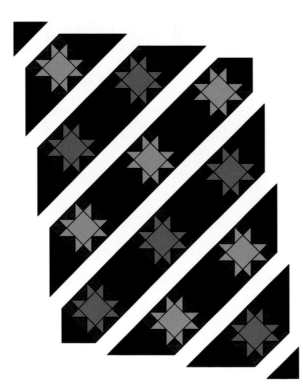

2. Sew the 2½" x 26" rust inner-border strips to the top and bottom edges of the quilt center. Sew the 2½" x 38½" rust inner-border strips to the sides of the quilt center.

3. Sew the 4½" x 30" dark purple outer-border strips to the top and bottom edges of the quilt center. Sew the 4½" x 46½" dark purple outer-border strips to the sides of the quilt center, completing the quilt top.

QUILTING AND FINISHING

1. Select the quilting designs from pages 108–127 that you wish to use in your quilt and mark them on your quilt top, referring to "Marking Quilting Designs" on page 28.

2. Referring to "Batting Options," "Backings," and "Layering and Basting" on page 29, layer and baste the quilt sandwich to prepare it for hand quilting.

3. Quilt the marked designs by hand, referring to "Hand Quilting" on page 30.

4. Referring to "Binding a Quilt" on page 31, bind the edges of the quilt.

5. Referring to "Finishing Touches" on page 33, add a hanging sleeve and a label to the back side of the quilt.

Wisdom is shared across generations. Many of life's lessons are learned at the elbows of mothers and grandmothers.

Rachel Thomas Pellman, 2001, Lancaster, Pennsylvania, 38" x 46".

◆

Unlike Lancaster County quiltmakers, midwestern Amish women felt free to use yellows and golds as part of their quiltmaking color palettes. Here, a gold background highlights the more subdued Monkey Wrench blocks. A commonly used fan quilting design fills the outer border.

May 21, 1950

"Tulips are in full bloom and can be seen in most any lawn and garden. Dogwood trees are also blooming, which is a sure sign for warmer weather. Farmers are planting corn and some people aren't finished cleaning house yet."

—From the *Budget*

FABRICS AND SUPPLIES

(fabric 42" wide after prewashing)

♦ ¾ yd. purple solid for inner border and Monkey Wrench blocks

♦ ¾ yd. dark green solid for Monkey Wrench blocks and binding

♦ 1⅜ yds. gold solid for plain blocks, side setting and corner triangles, and outer border

♦ 1⅜ yds. fabric for backing

♦ 42" x 50" piece of batting

CUTTING LIST

All cutting measurements include ¼" seam allowances.

From the purple solid, cut:

♦ 2 strips, each 2½" x 26", for inner border

♦ 2 strips, each 2½" x 38½", for inner border

♦ 12 strips, each 1½" x 11", for Monkey Wrench blocks.

♦ 24 squares, each 2⅞" x 2⅞", for Monkey Wrench blocks

From the dark green solid, cut:

♦ 12 strips, each 1½" x 11", for Monkey Wrench blocks

♦ 24 squares, each 2⅞" x 2⅞", for Monkey Wrench blocks

♦ 12 squares, each 2½" x 2½", for Monkey Wrench blocks

♦ 2 strips, each 2½" x 42", for binding

♦ 4 strips, each 2½" x 28", for binding

From the gold solid, cut:

♦ 2 strips on the lengthwise grain, each 4½" x 30", for outer border

♦ 2 strips on the lengthwise grain, each 4½" x 46½", for outer border

♦ 6 squares, each 6½" x 6½", for plain blocks

♦ 3 squares, each 10½" x 10½". Cut each of these squares diagonally in both directions to create side setting triangles. There will be 2 triangles left over.

♦ 2 squares, each 5½" x 5½". Cut each of these squares in half diagonally to create 4 corner triangles.

PIECING THE MONKEY WRENCH BLOCKS

1. Pair the 1½" x 11" purple strips with the 1½" x 11" dark green strips, right sides together. Sew the pairs of strips together lengthwise, using a ¼" seam allowance. Make 12 strip sets. Press the seam allowances toward the lighter fabric.

Make 12.

2. Cut the strip sets from step 1 into four 2½"-wide segments each, for a total of 48 segments.

3. Sew a segment from step 2 to the top and bottom edges of each of the twelve 2½" x 2½" dark green squares. You will use 24 of the segments from step 2.

Make 12.

4. Place a 2⅞" dark green and a 2⅞" purple square right sides together, with the edges precisely aligned. Cut this pair of squares in half diagonally to create 2 triangle pairs. Sew the triangle pairs together along the diagonal edges, taking care not to stretch the fabric. Press the seams toward the lighter fabric.

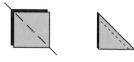

5. Repeat step 4 to make a total of 48 triangle-square units.

Make 48.

6. Sew a triangle-square unit to each end of a step 2 segment, positioning the triangles as shown. Repeat to make a total of 12 of these units.

Make 12.

7. Sew a unit from step 6 to opposite sides of a unit from step 3, completing the Monkey Wrench block. Make a total of 12 Monkey Wrench blocks.

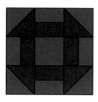

Make 12.

ASSEMBLING THE QUILT TOP

1. Referring to the diagram on page 89, join the Monkey Wrench and the 6½" x 6½" gold plain blocks together to create diagonal rows as shown. Add the gold side setting triangles, matching the right angle of the triangle to the side of the adjacent Monkey Wrench block. When you add the gold corner triangles, align the center of the corner triangle with the center of the adjacent Monkey Wrench block. Sew the rows together to complete the quilt center. Trim away any excess fabric from the

side and corner triangles, making sure to allow for the ¼" seam allowance on all 4 sides of the quilt center.

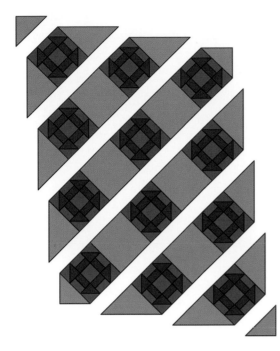

2. Sew the 2½" x 26" purple inner-border strips to the top and bottom edges of the quilt center. Sew the 2½" x 38½" purple inner-border strips to the sides of the quilt center.

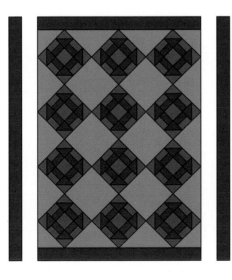

3. Sew a 4½" x 30" gold outer-border strip to the top and bottom edges of the quilt center. Sew the 4½" x 46½" gold outer-border strips the sides of the quilt center, completing the quilt top.

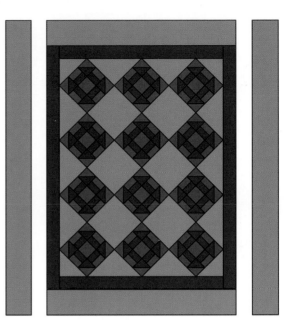

QUILTING AND FINISHING

1. Select the quilting designs from pages 108–127 that you wish to use in your quilt and mark them on your quilt top, referring to "Marking Quilting Designs" on page 28.

2. Referring to "Batting Options," "Backings," and "Layering and Basting" on page 29, layer and baste the quilt sandwich to prepare it for hand quilting.

3. Quilt the marked designs by hand, referring to "Hand Quilting" on page 30.

4. Referring to "Binding a Quilt" on page 31, bind the edges of the quilt.

5. Referring to "Finishing Touches" on page 33, add a hanging sleeve and a label to the back side of the quilt.

SHOOFLY

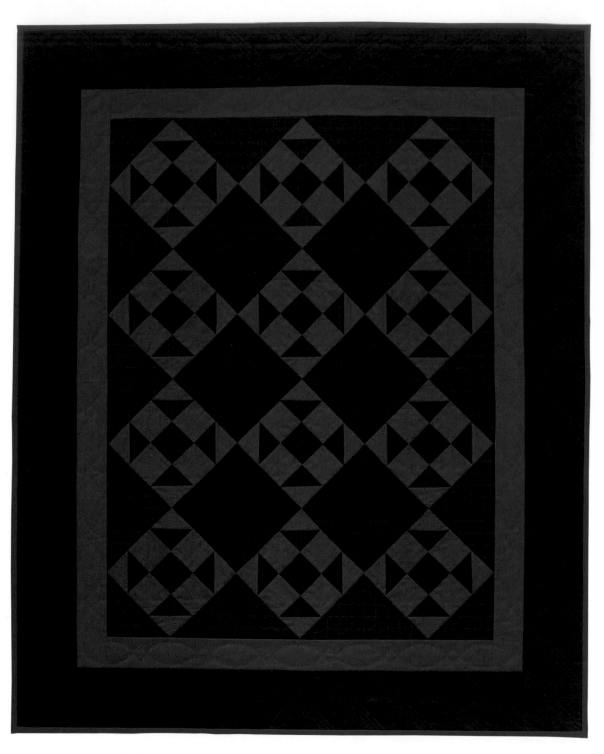

Rachel Thomas Pellman, 2001, Lancaster, Pennsylvania, 38" x 46".
Quilted by Elaine W. Good.

There is drama and intrigue in the simple, two-color Shoofly pattern. Except for the cable design in the inner border, all of the quilting is a series of straight lines.

April 29, 1950

"Most of the farming was done before the rain, so the men folks are doing other necessary work, shearing sheep, etc. The rainy spell also gives the women folks a chance to catch up on sewing."

—From the *Budget*

FABRICS AND SUPPLIES

(fabric 42" wide after prewashing)

♦ 1⅛ yds. blue solid for Shoofly blocks, inner border, and binding

♦ 1⅜ yds. black solid for Shoofly blocks, plain blocks, and outer border

♦ 1⅜ yds. fabric for backing

♦ 42" x 50" piece of batting

CUTTING LIST

All cutting measurements include ¼" seam allowances.

From the blue solid, cut:

♦ 48 squares, each 2½" x 2½", for Shoofly blocks

♦ 24 squares, each 2⅞" x 2⅞", for Shoofly blocks

♦ 2 strips, each 2½" x 26", for inner border

♦ 2 strips, each 2½" x 38½", for inner border

♦ 2 strips, each 2½" x 42", for binding

♦ 4 strips, each 2½" x 28", for binding

From the black solid, cut:

♦ 2 strips on the lengthwise grain, each 4½" x 30", for outer border

♦ 2 strips on the lengthwise grain, each 4½" x 46½", for outer border

♦ 6 squares, each 6½" x 6½", for plain blocks

♦ 3 squares, each 10½" x 10½". Cut each of these squares diagonally in both directions to create side setting triangles. There will be 2 triangles left over.

♦ 2 squares, each 5½" x 5½". Cut each of these squares in half diagonally to create corner triangles.

♦ 12 squares, each 2½" x 2½", for Shoofly blocks

♦ 24 squares, each 2⅞" x 2⅞", for Shoofly blocks

PIECING THE SHOOFLY BLOCKS

1. Pair the twenty-four 2⅞" x 2⅞" blue squares with the twenty-four 2⅞" x 2⅞" black squares, right sides together. Cut the squares in half diagonally to create triangle pairs. Sew the triangle pairs together along the diagonal edges, taking care not to stretch the fabric. Press seam allowances toward the darker fabric. Trim away excess points. Make a total of 48 triangle-square units.

Make 48.

2. Sew 2½" x 2½" blue squares to opposite sides of a 2½" x 2½" black square. Repeat to make a total of 12 of these units.

Make 12.

3. Sew a triangle-square unit to opposite sides of a 2½" x 2½" blue square. Repeat to make a total of 24 of these units.

Make 24.

4. Sew 2 units from step 3 to each side of a unit from step 2, completing the Shoofly block. Repeat to make a total of 12 Shoofly blocks.

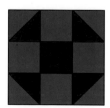

Make 12.

ASSEMBLING THE QUILT TOP

1. Referring to the diagram below, join the Shoofly blocks and the 6½" x 6½" black plain blocks together to create diagonal rows as shown. Add the black side setting triangles, matching the right angle of each triangle to the side of the adjacent Shoofly block. When you add the corner triangles, align the center of each corner triangle with the center of the adjacent Shoofly blocks. Sew the rows together to complete the quilt center. Trim away any excess fabric from the side setting and corner triangles, making sure to allow for the ¼" seam allowance on all 4 sides of the quilt center.

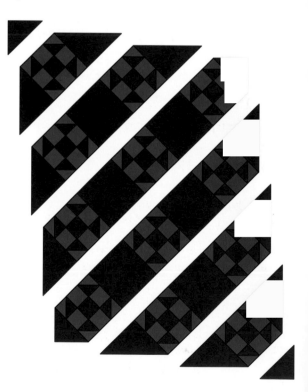

2. Sew the 2½" x 26" blue inner-border strips to the top and bottom edges of the quilt center. Sew the 2½" x 38½" blue inner-border strips to the sides of the quilt center.

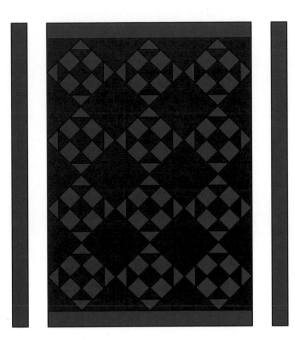

3. Sew the 4½" x 30" black outer-border strips to the top and bottom edges of the quilt center. Sew the 4½" x 46½" black outer-border strips to the sides of the quilt center, completing the quilt top.

QUILTING AND FINISHING

1. Select the quilting designs from pages 108–127 that you wish to use in your quilt and mark them on your quilt top, referring to "Marking Quilting Designs" on page 28.

2. Referring to "Batting Options," "Backings," and "Layering and Basting" on page 29, layer and baste the quilt sandwich to prepare it for hand quilting.

3. Quilt the marked designs by hand, referring to "Hand Quilting" on page 30.

4. Referring to "Binding a Quilt" on page 31, bind the edges of the quilt.

5. Referring to "Finishing Touches" on page 33, add a hanging sleeve and a label to the back side of the quilt.

MIFFLIN COUNTY QUILTS

*One-room schoolhouses provide for Amish education. Following completion of eighth grade,
formal education is discontinued and life's lessons are learned through experience.*

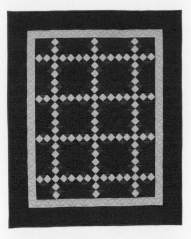

FOUR PATCH

NINE PATCH IN
BLOCKWORK

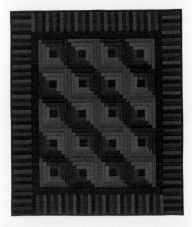

LOG CABIN

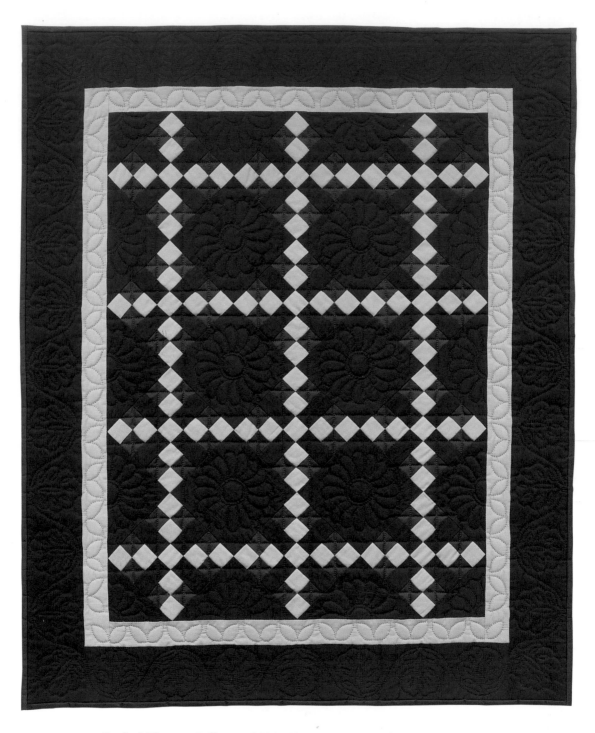

Rachel Thomas Pellman, 2001, Lancaster, Pennsylvania, 38" x 47".
Quilted by Rachel Lapp.

♦

Mifflin County quiltmakers often made variations on simple Four Patch or Nine Patch blocks.
Here, the Four Patch blocks are arranged to create a chain across the surface of the quilt.
The Mulberry Leaf quilting design on the border is distinctive to Mifflin County quilts.

August 8, 1935

"Work among the women folks is cooking for threshers and planting their early fall gardens and taking their matured vegetables in store for winter use."

—From the book *I Read It in the Budget* by Elmer S. Yoder

FABRICS AND SUPPLIES

(fabric 42" wide after prewashing)

- ¾ yd. tan solid for Four Patch blocks and inner border
- ¾ yd. brown solid for Four Patch blocks and binding
- 1½ yds. dark blue solid for rectangles between Four Patch blocks, plain blocks, and outer border
- 1⅜ yds. fabric for backing
- 42" x 51" piece of batting

CUTTING LIST

All cutting measurements include ¼" seam allowances.

From the tan solid, cut:

- 2 strips, each 2¼" x 26¾", for inner border
- 2 strips, each 2¼" x 39¾", for inner border
- 12 squares, each 1¾" x 1¾", for Four Patch blocks
- 12 strips, each 1¾" x 15", for Four Patch blocks

From the brown solid, cut:

- 12 strips, each 1¾" x 15", for Four Patch blocks
- 2 strips, each 2½" x 42", for binding
- 4 strips, each 2½" x 28", for binding

From the dark blue solid, cut:

- 2 strips on the lengthwise grain, each 4½" x 30¾", for outer border
- 2 strips on the lengthwise grain, each 4½" x 47½", for outer border
- 6 squares, each 6¾" x 6¾", for plain blocks
- 48 rectangles, each 1¾" x 3", for Four Patch blocks
- 3 squares, each 10⅛" x 10⅛". Cut each of these squares diagonally in both directions to create 10 side setting triangles. There will be 2 triangles left over.
- 2 squares, each 5⅜" x 5⅜". Cut each of these squares in half diagonally to create 4 corner triangles.

PIECING THE FOUR PATCH BLOCKS

1. Pair the 1¾" x 15" tan strips with the 1¾" x 15" brown strips, right sides to-gether. Sew the pairs of strips together lengthwise. Press the seam allowances toward the darker fabric.

Make 12.

2. Cut each strip set into 8 segments, each 1¾" wide, for a total of 96 segments.

3. Sew 2 segments together, alternating colors, to create a four-patch unit. Repeat to make a total of 48 of these four-patch units.

Make 48.

4. Sew a 1¾" x 3" dark blue rectangle between 2 four-patch units. Repeat to make a total of 24 of these units.

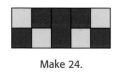

Make 24.

5. Sew a 1¾" x 3" dark blue rectangle to oppo-site sides of a 1¾" x 1¾" tan square. Repeat to make a total of 12 of these units.

Make 12.

6. Sew a unit from step 5 between 2 units from step 4, completing the Four Patch block. Re-peat to make a total of 12 Four Patch blocks.

Make 12.

ASSEMBLING THE QUILT TOP

1. Referring to the diagram, join the Four Patch and the 6¾" x 6¾" dark blue plain blocks together to create diagonal rows as shown. Add the dark blue side setting triangles, matching the right angle of the triangle to the side of the adjacent Four Patch block. When you add the dark blue corner triangles, align the center of the corner triangle with the

center of the adjacent Four Patch block. Sew the rows together to complete the quilt center. Trim away any excess fabric from the side setting and corner triangles, making sure to allow for the ¼" seam allowance on all 4 sides of the quilt center.

2. Sew the 2¼" x 26¾" tan inner-border strips to the top and bottom edges of the quilt center. Sew the 2¼" x 39¾" tan inner-border strips to the sides of the quilt center.

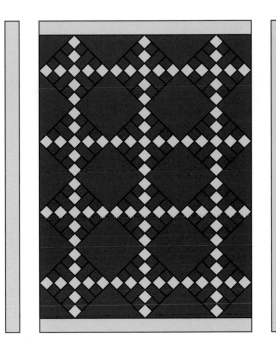

3. Sew each of the 4½" x 30¾" dark blue outer-border strips to the top and bottom edges of the quilt center. Sew the 4½" x 47½" dark blue outer-border strips to the sides of the quilt center, completing the Four Patch quilt top.

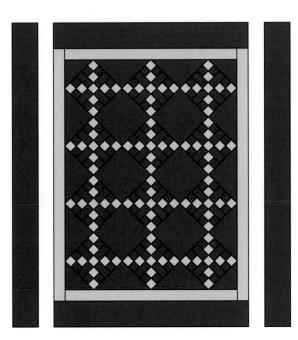

QUILTING AND FINISHING

1. Select the quilting designs from pages 108–127 that you wish to use in your quilt and mark them on your quilt top, referring to "Marking Quilting Designs" on page 28.

2. Referring to "Batting Options," "Backings," and "Layering and Basting" on page 29, layer and baste the quilt sandwich to prepare it for hand quilting.

3. Quilt the marked designs by hand, referring to "Hand Quilting" on page 30.

4. Referring to "Binding a Quilt" on page 31, bind the edges of the quilt.

5. Referring to "Finishing Touches" on page 33, add a hanging sleeve and a label to the back side of the quilt.

Rachel Thomas Pellman, 2001, Lancaster, Pennsylvania, 38" x 47".
Quilted by Rachel Lapp.

For variation, Mifflin County Amish women often surrounded Nine Patch blocks with more patchwork. In this example, additional rectangles and corner squares in the same colors unify and connect the individual scrappy Nine Patch blocks.

April 9, 1951

"On last Thursday . . . [we] went to our son, Jake Zooks, near Hotman's Station to help quilt and the men helped with carpenter work."

—From the *Budget*

FABRICS AND SUPPLIES

(fabric 42" wide after prewashing)
- 6" x 9" pieces of 12 different solid-colored fabrics for Nine Patch blocks
- ⅜ yd. medium blue solid for blockwork around Nine Patch blocks
- ¼ yd. magenta solid for blockwork around Nine Patch blocks
- ⅝ yd. green solid for plain blocks and side setting and corner triangles
- ⅓ yd. light blue solid for inner border
- 1⅜ yds. dark green solid for outer border
- ½ yd. dark brown solid for binding
- 1⅜ yds. fabric for backing
- 42" x 51" piece of batting

CUTTING LIST

All cutting measurements include ¼" seam allowances.

From the medium blue solid, cut:
- 48 rectangles, each 1¾" x 4¼", for blockwork

From the magenta solid, cut:
- 48 squares, each 1¾" x 1¾", for blockwork

From the green solid, cut:
- 6 squares, each 6¾" x 6¾", for plain blocks
- 3 squares, each 10⅛" x 10⅛". Cut each of these squares diagonally in both directions to create 10 side setting triangles. There will be 2 triangles left over.
- 2 squares, each 5⅜" x 5⅜". Cut each of these squares in half diagonally to create 4 corner triangles.

From the light blue solid, cut:
- 2 strips, each 2¼" x 26¾", for inner border
- 2 strips, each 2¼" x 39¾", for inner border

From the dark green solid, cut:
- 2 strips on the lengthwise grain, each 4½" x 30¾", for outer border
- 2 strips on the lengthwise grain, each 4½" x 47½", for outer border

From the dark brown solid, cut:
- 2 strips, each 2½" x 42", for binding
- 4 strips, each 2½" x 28", for binding

PIECING THE BLOCKS AND BLOCKWORK

1. Divide the twelve 6" x 9" pieces into 6 pairs featuring contrasting colors. From 1 fabric in the first pair, cut two 1¾" x 8" strips and one 1¾" x 4" strip. From the other fabric in the first pair, cut one 1¾" x 8" strip and two 1¾" x 4" strips. Set the 1¾" x 4" strips aside. Sew the three 1¾" x 8" strips together so that the same fabric lies on either side of the center strip. Repeat with the remaining 5 pairs to make a total of 6 of these strip sets. Cut each strip set into four 1¾"-wide segments.

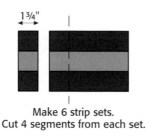

Make 6 strip sets.
Cut 4 segments from each set.

2. Sew the 1¾" x 4" strips from step 1 together, with the colors in the reverse order from the strip sets made in step 1. Make a total of 6 of these strip sets. Cut each strip set into two 1¾"-wide segments.

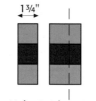

Make 6 strip sets.
Cut 2 segments from each set.

3. Sew a segment from step 2 between 2 segments from step 1 to create a Nine Patch block (the 2 colors of the segments should be the same). Make a second Nine Patch block with the remaining segments in the same colors.

4. Repeat steps 1–3 for the remaining fabric pairs to make a total of 12 Nine Patch blocks.

5. Sew a 1¾" x 4¼" medium blue rectangle to the top and bottom edges of each Nine Patch.

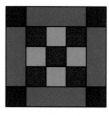

6. Sew a 1¾" x 1¾" magenta square to each end of the remaining 1¾" x 4¼" medium blue rectangles.

7. Sew a blockwork unit from step 6 to the sides of each Nine Patch block, completing the Nine Patch blocks and blockwork. Make a total of 12 Nine Patch blocks with blockwork.

Make 12.

ASSEMBLING THE QUILT TOP

1. Join the Nine Patch blocks (with blockwork) and the 6¾" x 6¾" green plain blocks to create diagonal rows as shown. Add the green side setting triangles, matching the right angle of each triangle to the side of the adjacent Nine Patch block (with blockwork). When you add the green corner triangles, align the center of the corner triangle with the center of the adjacent Nine Patch block (with

blockwork). Sew the rows together to complete the quilt center. Trim away any excess fabric from the side setting and corner triangles, making sure to allow for the ¼" seam allowance on all 4 sides of the quilt center.

2. Sew the 2¼" x 26¾" light blue inner-border strips to the top and bottom edges of the quilt center. Sew the 2¼" x 39¾" light blue inner-border strips to the sides of the quilt center.

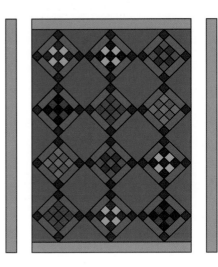

3. Sew the 4½" x 30¾" dark green outer-border strips to the top and bottom edges of the quilt center. Sew the 4½" x 47½" dark green outer-border strips to the sides of the quilt center.

QUILTING AND FINISHING

1. Select the quilting designs from pages 108–127 that you wish to use in your quilt and mark them on your quilt top, referring to "Marking Quilting Designs" on page 28.

2. Referring to "Batting Options," "Backings," and "Layering and Basting" on page 29, layer and baste the quilt sandwich to prepare it for hand quilting.

3. Quilt the marked designs by hand, referring to "Hand Quilting" on page 30.

4. Referring to "Binding a Quilt" on page 31, bind the edges of the quilt.

5. Referring to "Finishing Touches" on page 33, add a hanging sleeve and a label to the back side of the quilt.

LOG CABIN

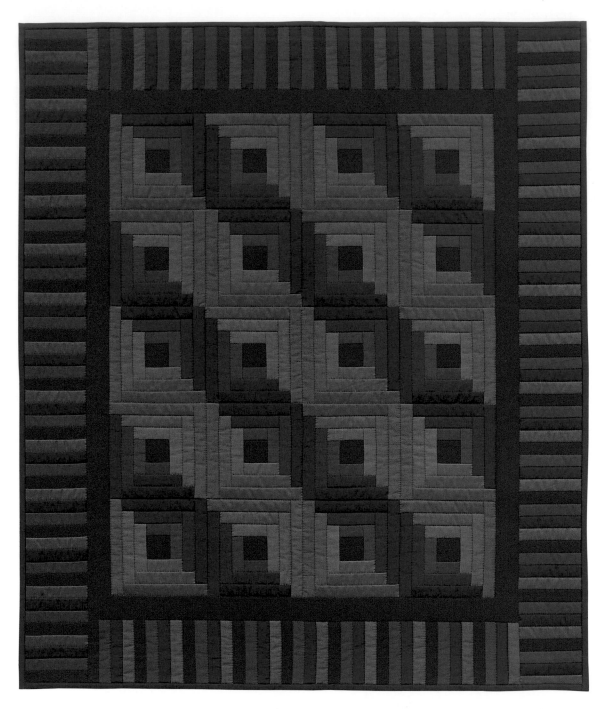

Rachel Thomas Pellman, 2001, Lancaster, Pennsylvania, 38" x 43".
Quilted by Rachel Lapp.

❖

There are some spectacular examples of Mifflin County quilters' elaborate Log Cabin creations.
The Log Cabin pattern was also a popular choice of Amish quiltmakers in the Midwest. To make a Log Cabin quilt
with a midwestern Amish look, simply adapt your colors to the midwestern Amish palette (page 22).

January 21, 1950

"The Junior Sewing Circle met at Levi Kramer's Wednesday evening to finish quilting a crib quilt. They were treated to ice cream and crackers after they finished the quilt."

—From the *Budget*

FABRICS AND SUPPLIES

(fabric 42" wide after prewashing)
- ⅓ yd. medium purple solid for logs #1 and #2 and outer border
- ½ yd. red solid for Log Cabin center squares, inner border, and outer border
- ⅓ yd. light brown solid for logs #3 and #4
- ¼ yd. dark purple solid for logs #5 and #6
- ¼ yd. medium brown solid for logs #7 and #8
- ⅞ yd. navy solid for logs #9 and #10, outer border, and binding
- ⅝ yd. dark brown solid for logs #11 and #12 and outer border
- 1¼ yds. fabric for backing
- 42" x 47" piece of batting

CUTTING LIST

All cutting measurements include ¼" seam allowances.

From the medium purple solid, cut:
- 20 strips, each 1¼" x 2", for log #1
- 20 strips, each 1¼" x 2¾" for log #2
- 46 strips, each 1¼" x 4½", for outer border

From the red solid, cut:
- 2 strips, each 2" x 24½", for inner border
- 2 strips, each 2" x 33½", for inner border
- 20 squares, each 2" x 2", for Log Cabin center squares
- 46 strips, each 1¼" x 4½", for outer border

From the light brown solid, cut:
- 20 strips, each 1¼" x 2¾", for log #3
- 20 strips, each 1¼" x 3½", for log #4

From the dark purple solid, cut:
- 20 strips, each 1¼" x 3½", for log #5
- 20 strips, each 1¼" x 4¼", for log #6

From the medium brown solid, cut:
- 20 strips, each 1¼" x 4¼", for log #7
- 20 strips, each 1¼" x 5", for log #8

From the navy solid, cut:
- 20 strips, each 1¼" x 5", for log #9
- 20 strips, each 1¼" x 5¾", for log #10
- 46 strips, each 1¼" x 4½", for outer border
- 2 strips, each 2½" x 42", for binding
- 4 strips, each 2½" x 28", for binding

From the dark brown solid, cut:
- 20 strips, each 1¼" x 5¾", for log #11
- 20 strips, each 1¼" x 6½", for log #12
- 46 strips, each 1¼" x 4½", for outer border

PIECING THE LOG CABIN BLOCKS

1. Sew a 1¼" x 2" medium purple log #1 to the top of a 2" x 2" red center square.

2. Working clockwise around the 2" red center square, add logs #2 through #12 in order, referring to the diagram for color placements. Make a total of 20 Log Cabin blocks.

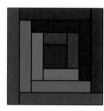

Make 20.

At work or at play, the Amish place a high value on the ability and opportunity to do things together.

ASSEMBLING THE QUILT TOP

1. Referring to the diagram, lay out the 20 Log Cabin blocks so that the colors create diagonal rows. Sew together 5 rows of 4 Log Cabin blocks each; then sew the rows of blocks together to complete the quilt center.

2. Sew the 2" x 24½" red inner-border strips to the top and bottom edges of the quilt center. Sew the 2" x 33½" red inner-border strips to the sides of the quilt center.

3. Sew the 1¼" x 4½" outer-border strips together in order—red, medium purple, navy, and dark brown—to create the outer border. Each of the top and bottom border strips require thirty-six 1¼" x 4½" strips. The side outer-border strips each require fifty-six 1¼" x 4½" strips. Sew the top and bottom border strips to the quilt center first. Sew the remaining 2 outer-border strips to the sides of the quilt center, completing the quilt top.

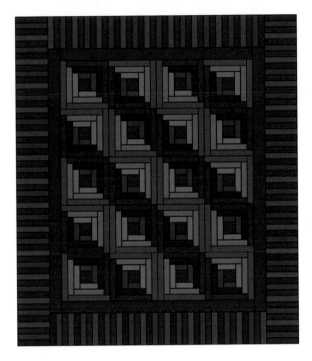

Quilting and Finishing

1. Select the quilting designs from pages 108–127 that you wish to use in your quilt and mark them on your quilt top, referring to "Marking Quilting Designs" on page 28.

2. Referring to "Batting Options," "Backings," and "Layering and Basting" on page 29, layer and baste the quilt sandwich to prepare it for hand quilting.

3. Quilt the marked designs by hand, referring to "Hand Quilting" on page 30.

4. Referring to "Binding a Quilt" on page 31, bind the edges of the quilt.

5. Referring to "Finishing Touches" on page 33, add a hanging sleeve and a label to the back side of the quilt.

QUILTING DESIGNS

The quilting designs on the following pages are grouped by the Amish region where each design is most typical. There are variations given for each area, and the designs are interchangeable on quilts within each region. Refer to "Marking Quilting Designs" on page 28 for additional marking instructions.

NOTE: Although the Lancaster County outer-border quilting designs will fit only the Lancaster County quilts, the midwestern and Mifflin County border designs are interchangeable and may be used accurately for quilts from both regions. The one exception to this is the Mulberry Leaf border design, which is distinctive to Mifflin County; this design would not be typical on a midwestern quilt.

LANCASTER COUNTY

Feather Star Medallion

SIZE: 12" circle (see page 110)
PATTERN: page 110

THE FEATHER STAR Medallion quilting design is commonly used in the middle of "Center Diamond" (page 36), but it can also be used effectively on the quilt "Bars" (page 40). Follow these steps to mark the design on these quilt tops.

1. Position the Feather Star Medallion design at the middle of the quilt top and mark the design.

Straight line

2. Referring to the diagram, mark a straight line from corner to corner in the center diamond, making sure that the line stays outside the area of the marked Feather Star Medallion design. Repeat to mark another straight line in the opposite corners, again making sure that the line stays outside the Feather Star Medallion design.

3. Referring to the diagram, mark parallel lines at ½" intervals on either side of the corner lines drawn in step 2.

4. Referring to the diagram, mark a line ½" in from the corner point of the center diamond and perpendicular to the lines marked in step 2. Continue marking parallel lines at ½" intervals until you reach 1" from the marked Feather Star Medallion design.

5. Use a series of pennies to draw half-circle scallop shapes along the lines outside the Feather Star Medallion design. To do this, lay some pennies on each marked line so that half of each penny lies above the line and half lies below it. Holding the pennies in place with your fingers as you go, mark around the top edge of each penny, creating a scalloped line. Repeat at each corner of the center diamond.

6. Also mark scallops along the seam line between the center diamond and the adjacent border, creating a hexagonal scalloped shape.

7. To fill the large triangles outside the center diamond, mark crosshatching lines at ¾" intervals.

8. To mark the Feather Star Medallion design on the quilt "Bars" (page 40), position the Feather Star Medallion design at the center of the quilt; then mark the design. Surround the Feather Star Medallion design with a series of tiny scallops in the same manner as for "Center Diamond," and fill the remaining spaces with ¾" crosshatching.

Center

Lancaster County Feather Star Medallion

*Rotate pattern around center
to complete motif.*

Feather Border

SIZE: appropriate for a 6¼"-wide border
PATTERN: pages 112–113

1. Place the diagonal line shown on the pattern at a 45° angle on the border corner, and begin marking the feather at the outer corner of each border. Work toward the border center.

2. Flip the design to mark it in the opposite direction on the adjacent border corner. Continue working toward the border center, making slight adjustments in the feathers if necessary.

Baskets Border

SIZE: appropriate for a 6¼"-wide border
PATTERN: page 114

1. Begin marking the baskets in the center of the border, and work toward the border corners. It will be helpful to mark the top and bottom lines of a series of baskets with one long ruler to ensure that the baskets will lie in a straight line on the border. Adjust the spacing between basket motifs as necessary to fill the space in your border.

2. Tip a basket motif diagonally to fill the border corners.

Pumpkin Seed Border

SIZE: appropriate for a 2"-wide border
PATTERN: page 115

1. Begin marking at the center of the border and work toward the corners, stopping the pumpkin seeds at the corner block.

2. Use the Small Flower Border Corner pattern (page 116) to fill the border corners.

Grapes and Grape Leaves Border

SIZE: appropriate for a 2"-wide border
PATTERN: page 115

1. Begin marking at the center of the border, and work toward the border corners.

2. Adjust the vine as necessary to turn the corner, and place a leaf or a bunch of grapes in the border corner blocks.

Small Flower Border Corner

SIZE: appropriate for a 2" x 2" border corner
PATTERN: page 116

Use this small flower for corner blocks on inner borders.

Feather Heart Corner Triangle

SIZE: appropriate for a 6¼" triangle
PATTERN: page 116

The Feather Heart quilting motif can be used for open triangles, or doubled and used to fill plain blocks.

Feather Wreath

SIZE: 8" circle
PATTERN: page 117

The Feather Wreath quilting design can be used in plain blocks. Half or one quarter of this motif can also be used in plain triangles.

Connect to Section B on page 113.

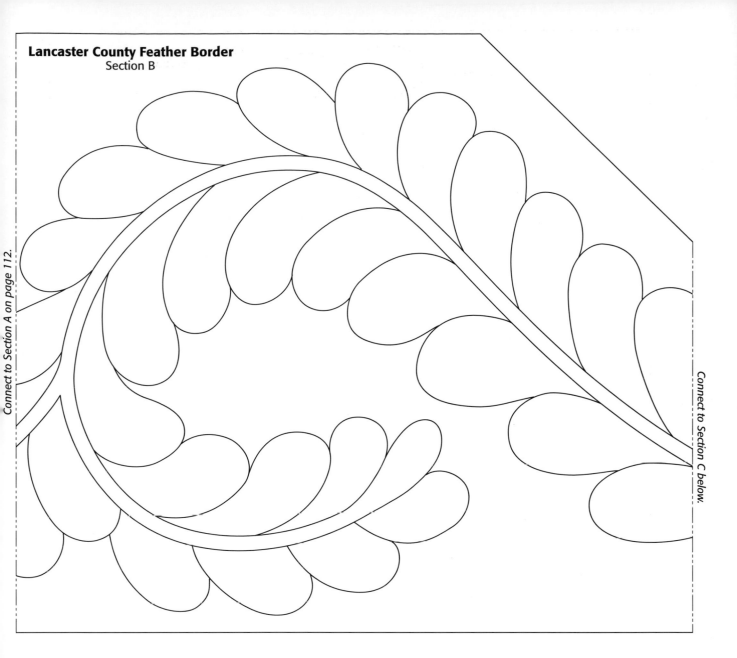

Lancaster County Feather Border
Section B

Connect to Section A on page 112.

Connect to Section C below.

Place this line at 45° angle on border corner and flip to complete pattern.

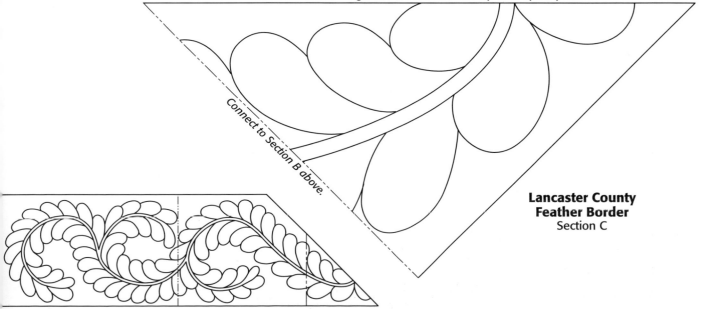

Connect to Section B above.

**Lancaster County
Feather Border**
Section C

Center

Lancaster County Baskets Border

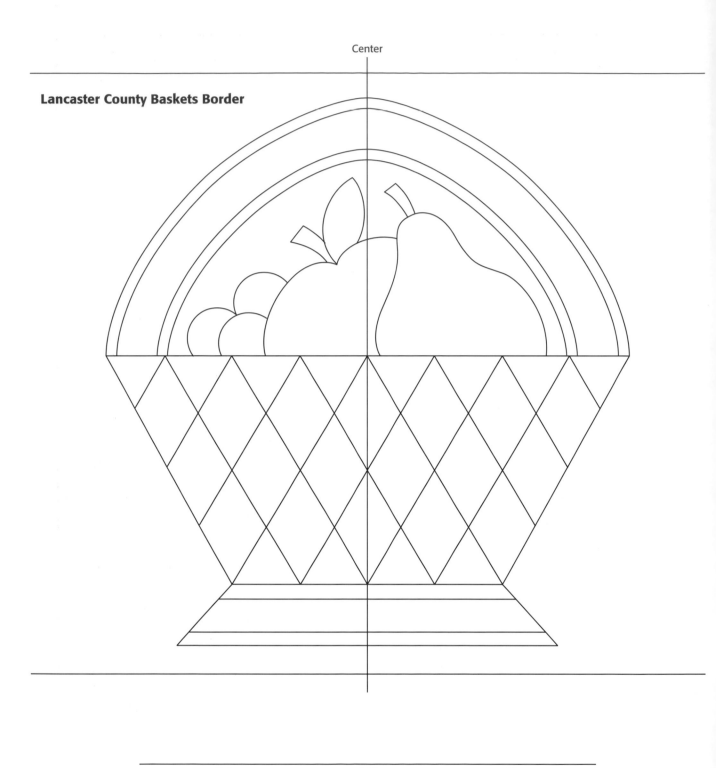

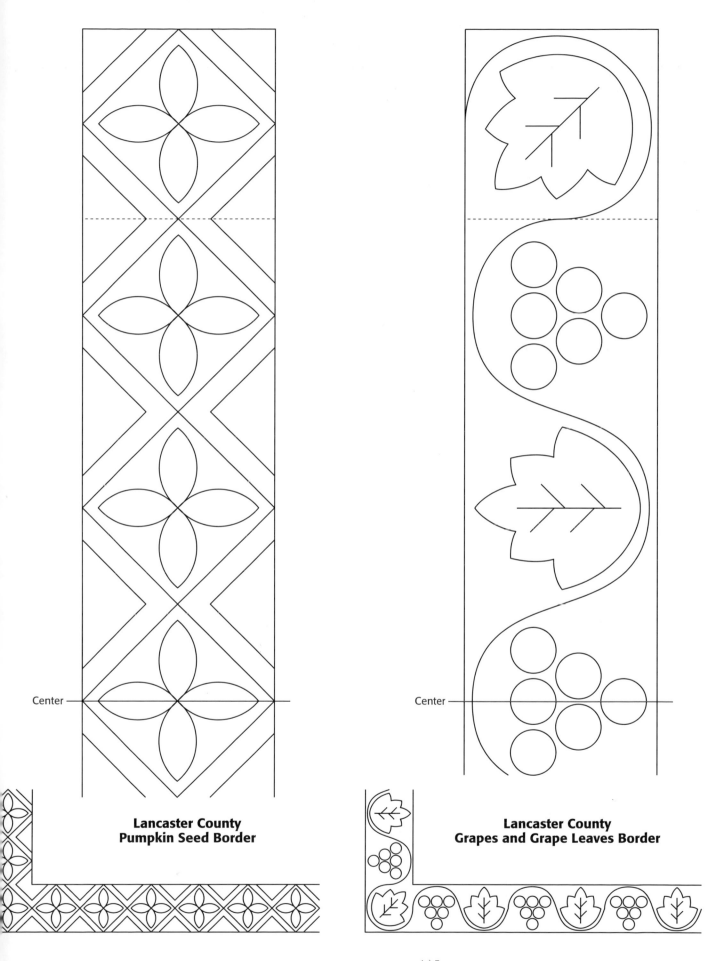

**Lancaster County
Pumpkin Seed Border**

**Lancaster County
Grapes and Grape Leaves Border**

Center

Center

**Lancaster County Feather Heart
Corner Triangle**

**Lancaster County Small Flower
Border Corner**

Center

Lancaster County Feather Wreath

MIDWEST

Cable Border
and Cable Border Corner

SIZE: appropriate for a 4"-wide border
PATTERN: pages 119–120

1. Begin marking the design at the center of the border, and work toward the border corners.

2. Extend or shorten the lines of the cable as necessary to meet the Cable Border Corner motif at each corner of the border.

Fan Border

SIZE: appropriate for a 4"-wide border
PATTERN: page 121

1. Begin by marking fans in each border corner.

2. Move the quilting design and mark fans from the center of the border outward to the corner areas. Mark the lines of the last fan so they meet the fan marked in the corner, making slight adjustments if necessary. Mark the lines of each fan all the way to the outer edges of the border so that the quilting lines will be sure to extend under the quilt binding.

Scallop and Diamond Border

SIZE: appropriate for a 2"-wide border
PATTERN: page 122

POSITION THE center of the design at the center of the border and begin marking toward the border corners. Adjust the design at the corner of your quilt, extending or shortening the lines as necessary to meet the lines on the adjacent border.

Crosshatch Feather

SIZE: 5½" circle
PATTERN: page 123

USE THIS Crosshatch Feather quilting motif in open spaces between pieced blocks. One half or one quarter of the feather can also be used in plain triangles.

Floral Feather

SIZE: 5½" circle
PATTERN: page 124

THIS FLORAL Feather quilting motif is also great for open spaces between pieced blocks. One half or one quarter of the motif can also be used in plain triangles.

Fancy Flower

SIZE: 3½" x 3½"
PATTERN: page 120

USE THE Fancy Flower quilting design in open spaces. It works nicely on "Ocean Waves" (page 68), where there is a lot of seam bulk in the center of the patches. To avoid quilting through numerous seam allowances, center the circle in this motif over the juncture of the seams in the middle of the Ocean Waves patches.

Center

Midwest Cable Border

Midwest Cable Border Corner

Midwest Fancy Flower

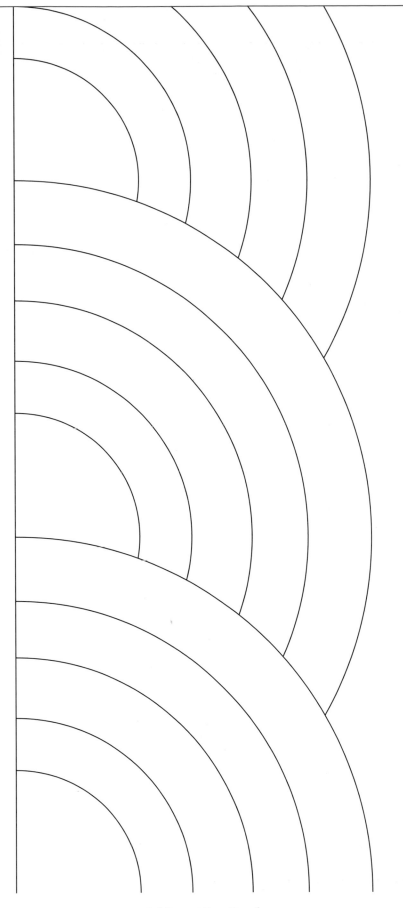

Midwest Fan Border

Center

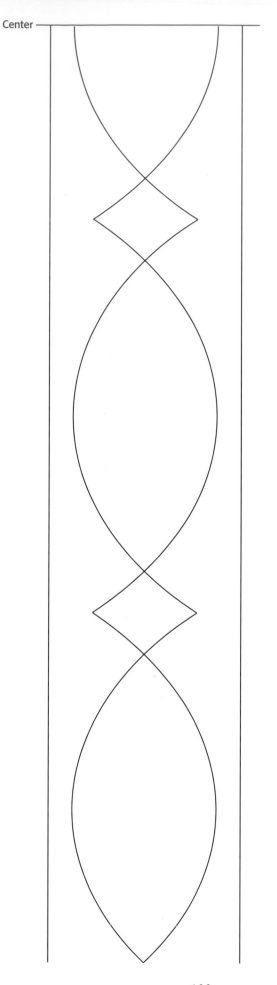

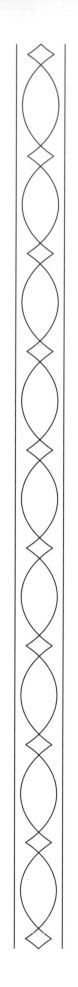

Midwest Scallop and Diamond Border

Midwest Crosshatch Feather

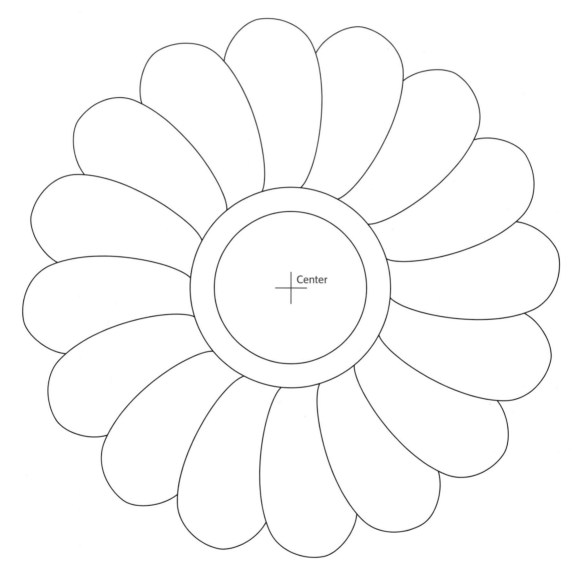

Center

Midwest Floral Feather

MIFFLIN COUNTY

Mulberry Leaf Border

SIZE: appropriate for a 4"-wide border
PATTERN: page 126

1. Begin marking this design at the center of the border, and work outward toward the border corners. Position the center leaf to face up on the side borders and down on the top and bottom borders.

2. Draw the vine into the border corners, and position a leaf on the diagonal in the corner block. Make slight adjustments as necessary.

Leaf Border

SIZE: appropriate for a 1¾"-wide border
PATTERN: page 125

BEGIN MARKING this design at the center of the border, and work outward toward the border corners. Mark the last leaf on each side of the border so that it meets the final leaf on the adjacent border at the corner. Make slight adjustments as necessary.

Scallop Circle

SIZE: 4¾" circle
PATTERN: page 127

USE THE scallop circle in plain blocks. One half or one quarter of the motif can be used to fill plain triangles.

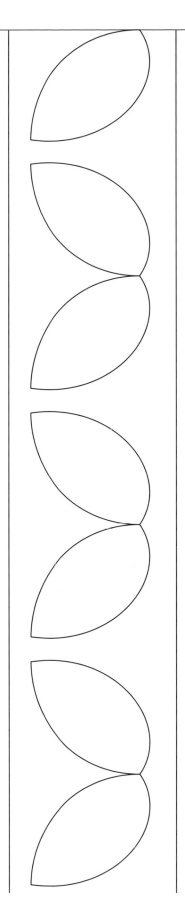

Center

Mifflin County Leaf Border

Center

Mifflin County Mulberry Leaf Border

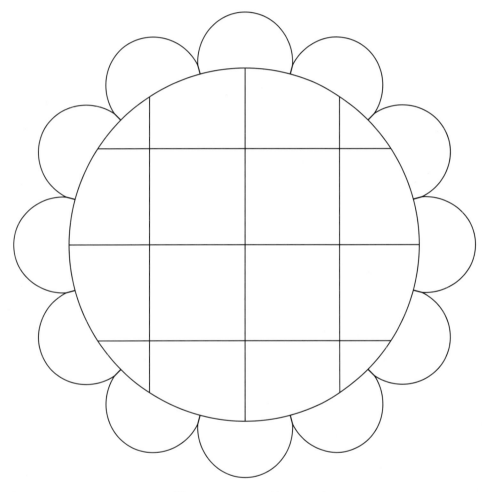

Mifflin County Scallop Circle

BIBLIOGRAPHY

Bishop, Robert, and Elizabeth Safanda. *A Gallery of Amish Quilts*. N.Y.: E. P. Dutton and Company, Inc., 1976.

Budget. Sugarcreek, Ohio, since 1890. The *Budget* is a weekly newspaper catering to the interests of Amish and Mennonite communities throughout North America. "Scribes" from the different areas submit news and information, which is compiled into a newspaper.

Good, Phyllis Pellman. *Quilts from Two Valleys*. Intercourse, Pa.: Good Books, 1999.

Granick, Eve Wheatcroft. *The Amish Quilt*. Intercourse, Pa.: Good Books, 1989.

Herr, Patricia T. *Quilting Traditions: Pieces from the Past*. Atglen, Pa.: Schiffer Publishing Ltd., 2000.

Hostetler, John A. *Amish Society*. Baltimore, Md.: The Johns Hopkins University Press, 1963.

Kraybill, Donald B. *The Riddle of Amish Culture*. Baltimore, Md.: The Johns Hopkins University Press, 1989.

Kraybill, Donald B., and Steven M. Nolt. *Amish Enterprise: From Plows to Profits*. Baltimore, Md.: The Johns Hopkins University Press, 1995.

Kraybill, Donald B., Patricia T. Herr, and Jonathan Holstein. *A Quiet Spirit*. Los Angeles, Calif.: UCLA Fowler Museum of Cultural History, 1996.

Pellman, Rachel, and Kenneth Pellman. *The World of Amish Quilts*. Intercourse, Pa.: Good Books, 1984.

———. *A Treasury of Amish Quilts*. Intercourse, Pa.: Good Books, 1990.

Yoder, Elmer S. *I Saw It in the Budget*. Hartville, Ohio: Diakonia Ministries, 1990.

ABOUT THE AUTHOR

RACHEL THOMAS PELLMAN has spent many hours in Amish homes, learning the stories of Amish women, the histories of their quilts, and researching current trends in Amish quiltmaking. She is the author of several quilt books, including *The World of Amish Quilts, A Treasury of Amish Quilts,* and *Tips for Quilters.* She lives in Lancaster County, Pennsylvania, with her husband, Kenny, and two teenage sons. She and Kenny own and operate Rachel's of Greenfield, a small company that designs and produces appliqué and pieced wall quilt kits available through retail shops nationwide.